teach® yourself

visual basic

mac bride

visual basic

mac bride

for over 60 years, more than
40 million people have learnt over
750 subjects the **teach yourself**
way, with impressive results.

be where you want to be
with **teach yourself**

The publisher has used its best endeavours to ensure that the URLs for external websites referred to in this book are correct and active at the time of going to press. However, the publisher has no responsibility for the websites and can make no guarantee that a site will remain live or that the content will remain appropriate.

For UK order enquiries: please contact Bookpoint Ltd., 130 Milton Park, Abingdon, Oxon OX14 4SB. Telephone: +44 (0)1235 827720. Fax: +44 (0)1235 400454. Lines are open 09.00–18.00, Monday to Saturday, with a 24-hour message answering service. Details about our titles and how to order are available at www.teachyourself.co.uk.

For USA order enquiries: please contact McGraw-Hill Customer Services, PO Box 545, Blacklick, OH 43004-0545, USA. Telephone: 1-800-722-4726. Fax: 1-614-755-5645.

For Canada order enquiries: please contact McGraw-Hill Ryerson Ltd, 300 Water St, Whitby, Ontario L1N 9B6, Canada. Telephone: 905 430 5000. Fax: 905 430 5020.

Long renowned as the authoritative source for self-guided learning – with more than 30 million copies sold worldwide – the *Teach Yourself* series includes over 300 titles in the fields of languages, crafts, hobbies, business, computing and education.

British Library Cataloguing in Publication Data: a catalogue record for this title is available from The British Library.

Library of Congress Catalog Card Number: On file.

First published in UK 2004 by Hodder Headline, 338 Euston Road, London, NW1 3BH.

First published in US 2004 by Contemporary Books, a Division of The McGraw-Hill Companies, 1 Prudential Plaza, 130 East Randolph Street, Chicago, Il 60601 USA.

This edition published 2004.

The 'Teach Yourself' name is a registered trademark of Hodder & Stoughton Ltd.

Computer hardware and software brand names mentioned in this book are protected by their respective trademarks and are acknowledged.

Copyright © 2004 Mac Bride

Typeset by MacDesign, Southampton

Printed in Great Britain for Hodder & Stoughton, a division of Hodder Headline, 338 Euston Road, London NW13BH by Cox & Wyman Ltd, Reading, Berkshire.

Hodder Headline's policy is to use papers that are natural, renewable and recyclable products and made from wood grown in sustainable forests. The logging and manufacturing processes are expected to conform to the environmental regulations of the country of origin.

Impression number   10 9 8 7 6 5 4 3 2 1

Year   2008 2007 2006 2005 2004

contents

preface

Visual Basic is one of the world's most widely-used programming languages. Its name is a reflection of its distant origins and not of its capabilities, for this Basic can be used to write very powerful and highly sophisticated applications. In its new .Net version, the language can be used to create stand-alone applications, ActiveX applets for Web pages or for WAP-enabled mobiles, or libraries of functions that can be called from other programs. As Visual Basic is fully compatible with the other programming languages in Microsoft's Visual Studio set, its programs can share data and functions with programs written in those languages.

The whole Visual Basic package is enormous – it comes on four CDs. Three of these contain the Help files, user guides, samples and other documentation. The complexity and sophistication of the language, and the thoroughness of the documentation can be daunting to the novice, but Visual Basic is pretty simple at heart. This book is intended for the novice, so I have tried to cut through the complexity and to focus on the essential structures and techniques. Some of the advanced features of the language are introduced, but only after a firm foundation has been built.

My aim is simple. I want to help you to master the essential tools and techniques, and to gain the confidence to explore the rest for yourself.

Mac Bride
2004

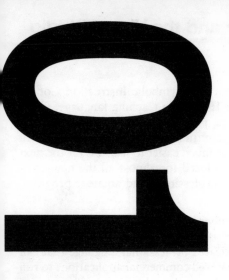

01

the visual studio

In this chapter you will learn:

- about the nature of Visual Basic.Net
- how to use the Visual Studio
- about the Toolbox and Properties windows
- how to get Help

1.1 Visual Basic and the Visual Studio

Visual Basic

BASIC – Beginners' All-purpose Symbolic Instruction Code – was first developed in the 1960s as a teaching language. Compared with other languages, programs written in it ran slowly and struggled with large quantities of data, but they were much easier to read and Basic was much easier to learn. Over the next 30 years, versions were produced for almost all the new computers and generations of professional and amateur programmers cut their teeth on Basic.

Visual Basic retains the keywords and coding structures of those early Basics, but is otherwise a completely different kettle of fish. This is a very sophisticated professional language that can be used to develop fully-featured commercial applications to run in Windows or on the Web.

There are two parts to any Visual Basic program. The 'Visual' part is the screen display – the *user-interface* in the jargon. This is assembled from ready-made components, such as buttons, text boxes and scroll bars, perhaps with the addition of image files brought in from outside the system. The 'Basic' part is the code, which processes data and alters the screen in response to the user's activity or other factors.

Event-driven programming

In earlier versions of Basic – or of any other programming language – the code would have been in a single file. It would have a single start point, though once started it would branch off into different routines, depending upon choices made or data entered. In Visual Basic, much of the code consists of more or less self-contained units attached to elements of the screen display, and these are activated by the user's interaction with those elements, e.g. clicking a button or entering text into a box.

The programs are *event-driven*. This makes programs easier to write – especially as the Visual Basic system handles the low level code which traps the events. You do not have to tell a button how to recognize that it has been clicked – you simply have to tell it what to do when it is clicked. Each block of code will typically perform a specific, limited task. It is usually possible to develop and debug each block of code largely independently – though keeping track of how changes in one part of a program can affect other parts is essential.

Code does not have to be attached to screen elements, but can be written into one or more separate, linked files. Here also, the code will normally be in discrete blocks, each designed for a particular function. In theory, and sometimes in practice, these blocks of code are reusable. Once you have written code to perform a task, you should never have to write it again, but can simply link its file into another program.

The .Net Framework

Like all the current generation of Microsoft languages, Visual Basic can be used to create Web applications within the .Net Framework. Amongst other things, this offers a common runtime environment (whichever language is used), access to data held in standard structures and the use of XML services. The big advantage of .Net to programmers is that it allows them to produce applications for the Internet without having to learn a new language.

Visual Studio

Visual Studio is the development environment, the window where you design, build and debug your programs. In its window, you have everything that you need for producing programs – apart from your own ingenuity and creativity. The ready-made screen elements and other objects are all at hand, ready to be dragged and dropped into place; options, properties and methods are all listed and can usually be set or selected with a couple of clicks. As Visual Basic is a large system, it makes life much easier to have its many features so accessible, but you should note that the Studio is a standard package which can also be used with other Microsoft programming languages, such as Visual Java and Visual C#. This has obvious advantages for programmers who work in several languages, but it does add to the size and complexity of the Studio environment.

1.2 Getting started

When Visual Studio opens, you are presented with the Start Page at the centre of multi-window (and we'll get back to those other windows shortly). It has three tabs, **Projects**, **Online Resources** and **My Profile**.

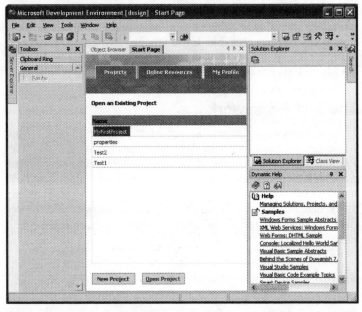

Figure 1.1 Visual Studio. The multiple window display works best on a large screen – this has been shrunk to fit on the page! Notice the Dynamic Help window at the bottom right – the topics listed here reflect what you are doing at the time.

Projects is the tab that you would normally use at start up, but when you are in Visual Studio for the very first time, you should go to **My Profile** so that you can customize the Studio.

My Profile

To set up Visual Studio for your work:

1 At the Start Page, click on the **My Profile** tab.

2 Drop-down the **Profile** list and select **Visual Basic Developer**.

3 Check that the other boxes are also set to **Visual Basic**.

4 Help can be displayed within Visual Studio (Internal) or in its own window (External) – click a radio button to set your preference.

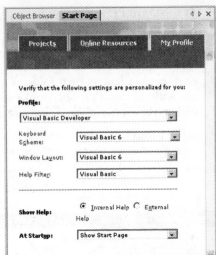

• If you change the Show help option, your PC will think very hard for several minutes while it reorganizes its Help files. Just wait for the update to finish.

Opening a project

A project is a set of files which will be turned into a program. If the sample files were included when Visual Basic was installed, you can use those to practise opening projects. They demonstrate a variety of programming techniques – though the code may not make much sense at first! (Look at them more closely later, when you have a reasonable grasp of the language.)

1 Click **Open Project**.

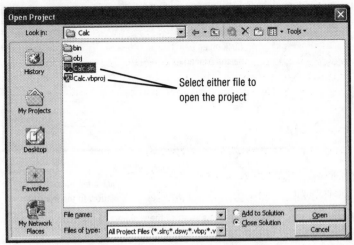

Select either file to open the project

2 At the **Open Project** dialog box, go to the **Look in** folder. To reach the sample, you probably need to work down through **Program Files > Visual Studio > VB > VB Samples** (or something similar, depending on your setup).

3 Each project has its own folder. Open it. You should find a file with an **.sln** (VB Solution) extension, and possibly one with a **.vbproj** extension. Select either of those and click **Open**.

◆ If the project has been used recently, it will be listed on the Start Page – simply click on the name to start.

Toolbox

Click on the name to open the set of tools

Form design and coding area

Solution Explorer

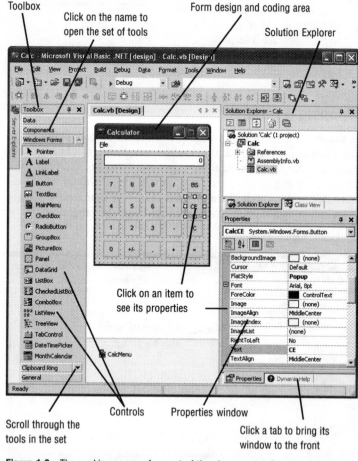

Click on an item to see its properties

Controls   Properties window

Scroll through the tools in the set

Click a tab to bring its window to the front

Figure 1.2 The working screen. As most of the elements can be moved, resized or hidden, yours may well not look quite like this.

4 At first, the central window will probably be empty. Look in the Solution Explorer (at the top right) for a file with a .vb extension. Double-click on this to open the project's form in the central window.

1.3 Arranging the windows

The Studio's screen display is infinitely flexible. You can open and close windows, resize them, lay them one on top of another, or set them floating anywhere on – or off – the Studio area.

Moving windows

A window can be moved by dragging on its title bar, or on its tab if it shares an area with another window. While you are dragging, the window is shown as an outline and the shape of this indicates how the window will fit into the display when you release it.

A window can be docked – fixed flush up against the frame – at the top, bottom, left or right of the Studio window. When the outline is in a docking area, it will align to the frame, showing you how it will fit.

If the docking area already has a window in it, the new window can share the space in three ways:

◆ Tiled one above the other, and sharing the space equally. The window will be placed above the existing one.

◆ Tiled side by side.

◆ Layered, one over the other, with a tab at the bottom for switching between the windows. When the outline is in the right position for layering, the tab will appear on it.

See Figure 1.3, overleaf.

If a window is already layered, dragging on the title bar moves the whole set of layered windows. Drag on the tab if you just want to move the one window.

If the outline is a simple rectangle, and not aligned to any part of the main frame, this will become a floating window.

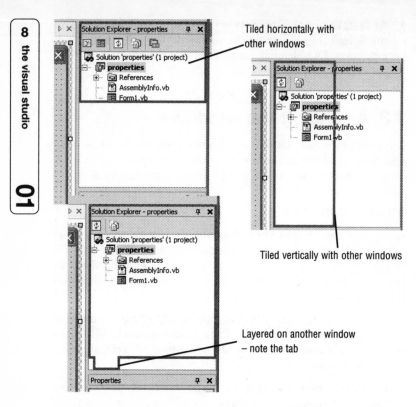

Figure 1.3 Outlines seen when moving windows over other ones.

Changing the size

Docked windows are more restricted. One docked at the left or right will occupy the full depth of the frame. You can change its width by dragging on its inner border. If there are two or more windows tiled in the docking area, they will together occupy the full depth and width of the area. You can change their relative sizes by dragging on the boundary between them. If you drag on the inner border, it affects the width of the whole docking area.

Windows docked at the top and bottom of the screen behave similarly – only their depth can be changed.

Floating windows can be resized freely. Point to any side or corner to get the double-headed arrow cursor, then drag to move the frame in or out.

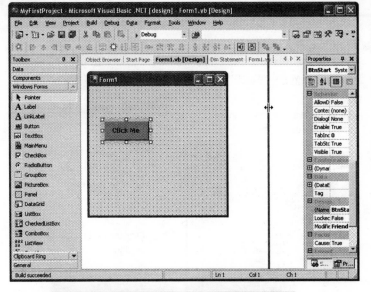

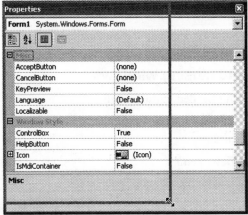

Figure 1.4 Changing the width of docked (top) and floating (bottom) windows. When the cursor is in the right place over a border, it changes to a double-headed arrow. Click and drag to move the border in or out.

Auto Hide

Auto Hide tucks windows out of the way when they are not in use. It is shown and controlled by the pin on the right of the title bar.

- When the pin is upright ⚲ Auto Hide is off and the window stays open. Click the pin to turn Auto Hide on.

- When the pin is on its side ⚲ Auto Hide is on and the window shrinks into the outer frame when not in use. To open a hidden window, point to its tab in the outer frame.

Auto Hide is on – when you click anywhere else on the screen, the window will close.

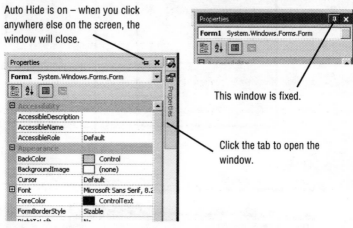

This window is fixed.

Click the tab to open the window.

Figure 1.5 Auto Hide – turn it on for those windows that you rarely use, and for other windows if you need more working space.

Opening and closing windows

If a window isn't needed, close it – click the **Close** button ⊠.

To reopen a window:

1 Open the **View** menu.

2 Click on the window to open.

Or

- Use the keyboard shortcuts – they are listed on the **View** menu.

Or

- Click the buttons in the Standard toolbar to open the Properties 🗗 or Toolbox 🗙 windows.

Restore the default display

If you get your display into a mess – and it's easily done – the simplest way to sort it out is to restore the default layout. Go to the Start Page in the central area of the screen, and open the My Profile tab. Select *Visual Basic 6* as the Window Layout. Click the Design button at the top of the central area to redisplay the form.

1.4 The Tools and Properties

When you are in design mode, with a form at the centre of the display, the Toolbox and Properties windows come into play.

The Toolbox

The **Toolbox** has five sets of tools. The Windows Forms set should be open – if it is not, then click on its name. This set contains *controls* – the Toolbox objects which you can place on

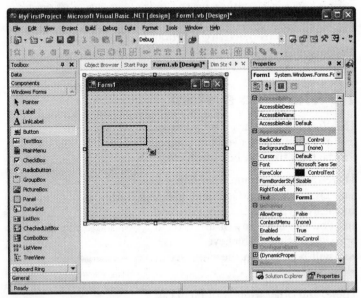

Figure 1.6 The screen while a control is being added to the form. Note the Toolbox and Properties windows.

the form to create the screen display of your program and/or to interact with its users. Some of these, such as the Button and the CheckBox will be familiar and have obvious purposes; others such as the Panel and ImageList will be less familiar.

The Properties window

On the right of the display, you should see the **Properties** window. All objects on a form – including the form – have properties which control their appearance and behaviour, e.g. the position and size, the background and foreground colours, if there is text, the font used and the text itself, whether the object is visible and/or enabled when it first appears.

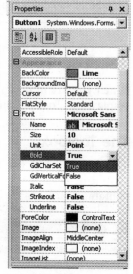

Different objects have different sets of properties, though many are common to all.

Properties can be set at design time, or during run time – either by the user's actions or from within the program. In fact, most onscreen activity is produced by changing properties.

1.5 The Help system

The Visual Studio has a very extensive and comprehensive Help system – in fact, its size can be a problem.

There are four ways into the Help system: Dynamic Help, Contents, Index and Search. Each has its own window, and you can have any or all of them open at any time. Whichever you use, you will be taken to the same set of Help pages.

These, and other aspects of Help can be reached through the Help menu.

Dynamic Help

This reflects what you are doing at the time. When you first start, it will offer help on the management of projects and similar getting-started topics. When you are laying out your forms, it will offer topics on the currently-selected control on a form; when you are writing code, it will offer Help on the methods and functions that you are using.

The Dynamic Help window is visible at the bottom right when you first start. Once a project is opened, it will be overlaid by the Properties window (in the default layout).

1   To read a topic, click on its link. The Help page will be displayed in the central area of the screen.

2   The Help page may contain links to related or more detailed topics – click on the links to reach the Help you need.

3   When you have done with the Help, click on the appropriate tab at the top of the central area to get back to where you were.

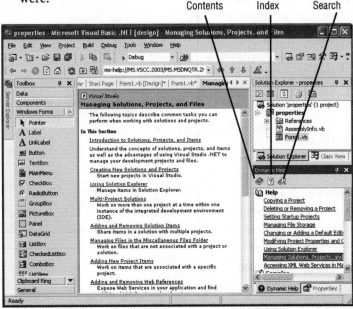

Figure 1.7   The Help page is displayed in the central area. It may contain links to other Help pages. Notice the icons at the top of the Dynamic Help window – these open the other Help windows.

Contents

This organizes the Help pages into a 'book', with chapters and sub-sections within them. It's a good way into the Help system when you first start – as you can get a good overview of what is available; and it is also useful when you know more or less what you need Help on, but don't necessarily know the right words.

Open the chapters to see the subsection names and topic titles, and follow up any that sound promising. You may need to go down two or three levels to reach a Help page – and even that may be mainly a list of links to other pages.

To use the contents:

1 Ensure that the **Filtered by** option is set to Visual Basic – so you only get the relevant Help pages!

2 Click ⊞ 🐜 to open a chapter or subsection.

3 Click ⊟ 🐜 to close a set if there is nothing there that you want.

4 Click the topic title or ▤ to open a Help page – it will be displayed in the central area.

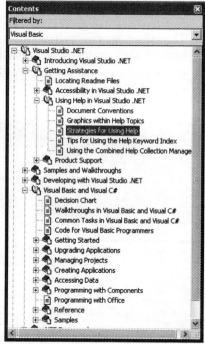

Figure 1.8 You can browse the Help system from the Contents window.

Help text size

The Help pages are displayed by your browser (normally Internet Explorer) running within the Studio. The size of the text depends upon the settings in your browser, and can only be changed from that application.

Index

If you know the words for what you are looking for, you will find it faster through the Index than through the Contents. This has an alphabetical list of all the significant words in the Help system. Use it to find Help on specific controls, properties and methods.

1 Type in the first few letters of a word. The Index will scroll through to that part of the list.

2 Select the index entry.

3 The Index Results window will open at the bottom of the screen. Select a topic to display it in the central area.

4 Close the Index Results window when it is no longer needed.

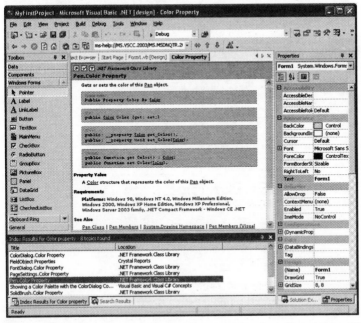

Figure 1.9 An index entry will typically produce a number of results, and some will be more relevant than others.

Search

Use this as an alternative to the Index for finding Help on specific words. As a search finds every reference to the given word, it will normally produce more results than the Index, though a higher proportion will be less relevant. There are four search options:

- **Search in titles only** will find fewer results, but they will be more relevant.

- **Match related words** will find singulars and plurals of the same word, e.g. look for 'checkbox' and it will also find 'checkboxes'.

- **Search in previous results** allows you to run a search in several stages, e.g. if you wanted to read about MDI forms (multiple document interface) and windows, you could search first for 'MDI forms' (finding 78 pages), then search within those pages for 'windows' (finding 14 pages).

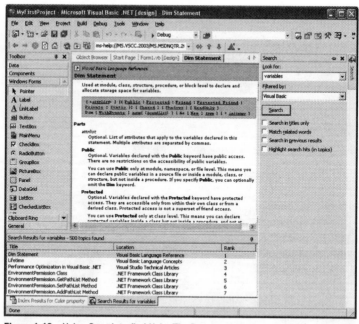

Figure 1.10 Using Search to find Help. The Results window can list up to 500 topics – but if you get this many and you can't see what you need in the top few, you may want to redefine your search.

• **Highlight search hits (in topics)** puts a blue background on the search words in the Help pages.

1.6 Online Resources

There is lots of Help, plus samples, updates and other resources available online, both at Microsoft's sites and elsewhere.

To explore the online Help:

1 In the central area, click on the Start Page tab then on the Online Resources tab.

2 If you are not already online, get connected now.

3 Browse through the resources using the navigation bar on the left, the tabs at the top and the links within the pages.

Or

4 Go to the **Search Online** page to find specific Help.

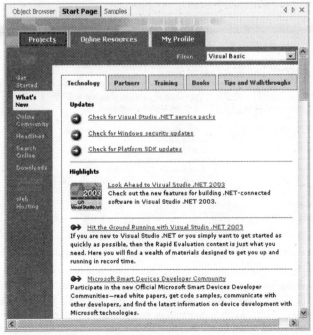

Figure 1.11 The Online Resources are well worth exploring – take half an hour to get an idea of what is around, then go back when you need its depth and range of assistance.

1.7 Options

The Studio can be customized to your tastes. Some of the options are largely cosmetic – e.g the fonts and colours that are used in the screen display – others have rather more impact on how you work.

Most should be left at their defaults until you have spent some time with the system. One or two are worth setting earlier on, and perhaps the most important is the projects location – the default folder for storing new projects.

To set the project location:

1 Open the **Tools** menu and select **Options...**

2 In the **Environment** folder, select **Projects and Solutions**.

3 For the **Visual Basic projects location** either click **Browse...** and locate the folder, or type the path to it.

4 Click **OK**.

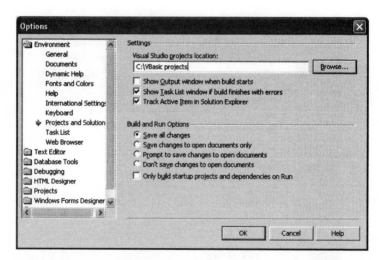

Figure 1.12 The **Options** dialog box. While you have it open, check that the **International Settings** are correct and that the **Keyboard** is set for Visual Basic. We'll come back to the **Fonts and Colors** when we start writing code. The settings in the other folders should be left at their defaults for the time being.

Summary

- Visual Basic is an object-oriented, event-driven language. This current version is one of several Microsoft languages that use the .Net framework.

- Visual Studio is the development environment for .Net languages.

- The Studio has separate windows for each aspect of its system. These can be arranged within or around the main window, whichever works best for you.

- The screen display of a program is created by placing controls on a form. The controls are selected from the Toolbox, and customized through the Properties window.

- There is an extensive Help system, which you can browse or search through. Additional Help is available at Microsoft's web site.

02

the basics of
visual basic

In this chapter you will learn:

- about object-oriented programming
- about controls and properties
- how to use the MsgBox( ) function
- about comments in code

2.1 A first application

The best way to learn is by doing, so let's get doing! This first application demonstrates some basic techniques of programming in Visual Basic – pared down to the absolute minimum. We will place a control on a form to create our visible user interface, then add code to respond to an event, and use a standard Windows component to output the result. Or, in plain English, we will set up a button which, when clicked, will display 'Ouch!'

Start the project

If you have a sample project open, close it down by using **File > Close**. If you are prompted to save any changes you have made, click **No** to decline the offer.

You can start a new project off from scratch, but in practice, you would normally start from one of the templates. These have some of the basic code and structures in place for creating different types of applications. For most of this book, we will start from the Windows Application template.

1 At the Start Page, go to the **Projects** tab and click **New Project**.

Or

+ Open the **File** menu, point to **New** and select **Project...**

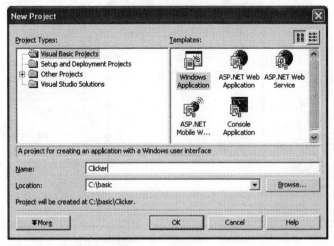

Figure 2.1 Starting a new project.

2 At the **New Project** dialog box, select the *Windows Application* template (in the *Visual Basic Projects* folder).

3 Enter a **Name** for the project – I've called this *Clicker*.

4 If you have not yet set your default project location in the Options (see page 18) – or you do not want to use this – select the **Location**.

5 Click **OK**.

♦ The Studio will create a new folder, with the set of core files and subfolders that the project needs. As this is a Windows application, a blank form will be placed in the working area.

Set up the form

The form is the space where you assemble the buttons, pictures, text areas and other controls to create the user interface. When the project is built into a program, the form becomes a window.

In this project, the form will contain a single button (at first,

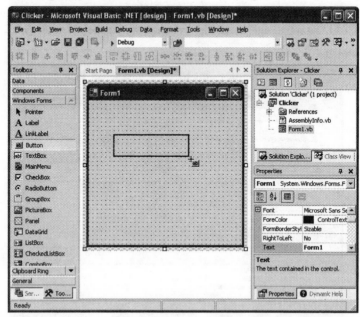

Figure 2.2 Adding a control. In this example, the button can go anywhere, but you would normally plan the layout carefully.

though we'll add another later). The Button control can be found in the Toolbox's Windows Forms set. This should be open when the project starts – if not, click on its name bar to open the set.

To draw any control, click where you want one corner to go and drag across to the opposite corner. A black outline will show you the size. Absolute accuracy is not essential. Controls can be moved or resized at any time.

1 In the **Toolbox**, select **Button**.

2 Click and drag on the form to draw a rectangle around 5 grid squares deep by 15 across.

3 In the Properties window, go to the Text field, delete 'Button1' and replace it with 'Click Me'.

Add the code

Code can be attached to controls, so that it is activated when an event occurs. We will be looking at this in detail in the next chapter. At this point, it is enough to know that buttons can respond to clicks – something you may be aware of already! When this button is clicked, a message will appear on the screen, using a standard Windows dialog box.

1 Double-click on the **Click Me** button.

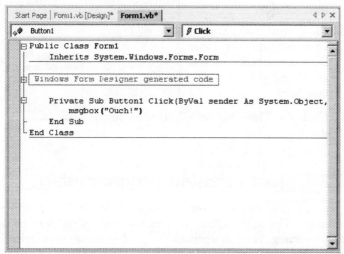

Figure 2.3 The code display.

2 The central area will display the code for the form – note that some is already in place. The cursor will be on a blank line beneath the line starting 'Private Sub Button1_Click(…)' Type in this – replace "Ouch!" by your own message:

```
msgbox("Ouch!")
```

3 That's it – the *program* is complete! All we have to do now is run it to see what it does. Open the **Debug** menu and select **Start** or press [**F5**].

4 There will be a slight delay while the system *builds* the application – converts the project into a program.

You should see your form appear, as a window.

Click the **Click Me** button. You should then see a little dialog box containing your message and an **OK** button.

5 Click **OK** to close the message box.

6 Click your button, read your message and close the message box until you get bored – it shouldn't take long.

7 Click the **Close** button [×] to shut down the application.

2.2 Object-oriented programming

Like most modern programming languages, Visual Basic is object-oriented. The approach is now established as the way to do programming. You can – generally – produce better, more reliable programs faster with an object-oriented language.

People write big books about the theory and practice of object-oriented programming. I'm going to spend a couple of pages on it, which should be enough to give you the main jargon and a working grasp of its principles. We'll come back to it from time to time, as necessary.

Traditional v. OO languages

First, let's look at the difference between a 'traditional' programming language and an object-oriented one. Think of a clickable button on a Windows screen. If you wanted to create this in a traditional language, you would have to write some code to draw the button on the screen, then write some more to track the mouse movement and watch for the click, and some more to draw the button as it is clicked, and then – at last – you can write the code to do the job called up by the click. Oh yes, and you'll have to do most of it again next time you want another clickable button!

Visual Basic *knows* about buttons. It knows what they look like and how they interact with mice. If you want a clickable button in a Visual Basic program, all you have to do is specify where to put it, what to write on it, and what to do when it is clicked.

In an object-oriented language, you have ready-made, reusable blocks of code and data – the objects.

The nature of objects

To understand the characteristics of objects, let's take a real world analogy. Think of a car. It has certain characteristics including its shape, colour, and speed and direction (when moving). In OO jargon, these are *properties*, which may be set at the time of creation and/or during the program's execution. It can also do things, and have things done to it, such as opening and closing doors, driving, turning, braking and/or crashing. An object's activities are controlled by *methods* – blocks of code. Some methods may be fully written already, so that you can simply utilize what's there to do a job. Some methods are little more than shells, containing only the code to link them to an event or property – it's then up to you to write the code for the activity. You can also rewrite or *override* the code of a fully written method if you need to modify its activity.

Where do objects come from? Let's go back to the car analogy. Cars are created to the pattern defined in a blueprint (actually, nowadays it will be a set of CAD files, but just bear with me on this) and you can produce as many as you need from the same blueprint. In OO programming, *classes* are the blueprints for objects. The car analogy breaks down a bit here, as both the class and the object are blocks of data and methods. The difference is that, for any single class, there can be any number of objects derived from it, or *instances* of it, to use the OO jargon.

An object takes on, or *inherits*, all the characteristics and code of its class, but you can change or add to them. You can define new classes of your own based on existing classes, and – as with objects – the new ones inherit the characteristics of the base class.

There's a lot more to object-oriented programming theory than this, but we'll come back to it as and when we need it. This is a practical book.

2.3 The Code window

When you get back to the Studio, you should be back where you were, with the code on view. If it isn't, double-click the *Click Me* button to display the code. Let's have a closer look at it – we'll take it from the top.

```
Public Class Form1
```

Here we have a class of our own. Our program will be built on a form – as are all Windows applications either in whole or in part – and so code is based on the *Form* class. It is given the default name of *Form1*.

The end of the code is marked by the line:

```
End Class
```

The form is a standard Windows object, and the system already has ready-written code to control all the usual things that forms can do or can have done to them.

```
Inherits System.Windows.Forms.Form
```

The 'Inherits…' line links our class (the code) to its base class. In 'System.Windows.Forms.Form' we see Visual Basic's naming convention at work. Things are identified by the names of the object or set to which they belong, with dots between the names. 'Form' is one of a number of components in the 'Forms' set, which belongs to the 'Windows' set, which is itself part of the 'System' body of code.

The next thing to note is that there is a lot more there than it seems. Notice the ⊞ icon beside the 'Windows Form Designer generated code' line.

```
⊞  Windows Form Designer generated code
```

Click it and see what happens.

The boxed line opens into a whole long block of code. As it says on the label, this is generated automatically by the system when the form is created and when you add controls to it. This is not something that you should fiddle with, but have a good look at it as it demonstrates some key points about programming in Visual Basic. Notice these lines in the last block of code.

```
Private Sub InitializeComponent( )
    Me.Button1 = New System.Windows.Forms.Button
```

Me in this instance is the form. **Button1** is the button you have just placed on it, and **New** is a *constructor* – it creates a new object (Button1) from a class (System.Windows.Forms.Button).

The button's definition follows shortly after. Notice that some properties are set by simply allocating values:

```
    Me.Button1.Name = "Button1"
```

But other properties are themselves objects and must be set up with **New**. This takes the Size definition from the System.Drawing class which – amongst other things – determines the measure to be used when giving sizes.

```
    Me.Button1.Size = New System.Drawing.Size(144, 40)
```

The form's definition has a similar mixture of constructors and assigned values.

```
    'Form1
    '
    Me.AutoScaleBaseSize = New System.Drawing.Size(5, 13)
    Me.ClientSize = New System.Drawing.Size(292, 266)
    Me.Controls.Add(Me.Button1)
    Me.Name = "Form1"
    Me.Text = "Form1"
```

Notice the line that places the button on the form:

```
Me.Controls.Add(Me.Button1)
```

This adds the button to the set of controls on the form. You can use similar expressions yourself to add controls at run time.

Let's move on. Click the ⊞ icon by the top line:

This will fold the code back into its boxed header line.

```
⊟ #Region " Windows Form Designer generated code "
```

```
Private Sub Button1_Click(By Val sender as System.Object ...
```

A *Sub* is a subroutine, which is a type of method. (The other type of method is a function, which we shall meet in Chapter 6.) This sub is activated when the button is clicked, and as this is a standard Windows operation, the framework of the code was generated automatically by Visual Basic.

There is a whole string of stuff in the brackets after the name. These are used to carry values into and out of the sub, and are known as *parameters*. As with other generated code, these should be left alone – the system needs them. (See Chapter 5 for more on parameters.)

Notice that your line of code has been tidied up. It should read:

```
MsgBox("Ouch!")
```

The keyword, *MsgBox*, has been given capitals at the very start, and at the start of the 'Box'. When the Visual Basic system finds the name of a method, function or property or any other kind of keyword, it imposes its standard capitalization style – all words have initial capitals; compound words have capitals at the start of each of their component words.

2.4 Controls and properties

Controls have properties which govern their appearance and behaviour. The properties vary, depending upon whether the control is a button, text box, scroll bar or whatever, but many of the same properties are found in all controls, and properties are set in a limited number of ways.

In this next example, we will explore how properties are set at the design stage and during the program's run. Close down the Clicker project and start a new one.

Placing the controls

We will be using three controls: Button, Label (which can display text) and TextBox (which can be used to display text or to accept text typed by the user). With all three we will change the name, text, colours and font.

1 Click the **TextBox** tool [abl TextBox] and draw a rectangle across the top of the form to create a TextBox there. It can only be one line deep – if you draw a deeper box, it will shrink back down – and should be long enough to hold half a dozen words. If necessary, drag on one of the side handles on the left or right to stretch it.

2 Click the **Button** tool [ab] Button] and create a button in the middle of the form.

3 Click the **Label** tool [A Label] and draw a rectangle at the bottom of the form, as wide as the TextBox, but deeper.

Setting properties

You can set the properties for each control as you put it into place, but it is often more efficient to get all the controls onto the form first, then set all the properties at once. The reason is this. Where the same property is to be set to the same *attribute* (value) on several controls, e.g. the same colour font, you can do it in a single operation. And even where a property has different values, it is quicker to set the same property for different controls than to set different properties on one control. You will see this when we give new names to the controls.

The **Name** property is set by typing in a new value.

1 Click in the TextBox to select it.

2 Scroll down towards the bottom of the Properties window until you find the **Design** set.

3 Click into the **Name** field. The default name will be *TextBox1*. Delete this and type in a new name which better describes what the TextBox will be used for, e.g. *UserInput*.

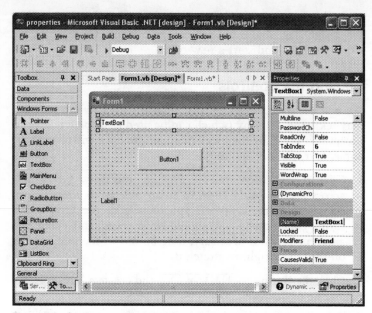

Figure 2.4 Starting to set the properties. I have expanded the Properties window to give easier access to its many fields.

4 Select the Button. Notice you don't have to hunt through the Properties window as the Name field will still be selected. Change its name to *CopyButton*.

5 Select the Label and change its name to *Output*.

The **Text** property defines what will be written on the controls. It can be set in the same way. Set the Text of the TextBox to 'Enter your text here', and of the Button to 'Copy'. Clear the Label so that it will appear blank when the program starts.

You will find **Text** in the Appearance set towards the top of the Properties window.

Now let's try setting the same property to the same value on several controls. First you have to select them. There are two ways to select a set of controls:

* Click and drag to draw a dotted rectangle over the controls – it only needs to enclose part of any control to select it.

* Hold down [**Shift**] and click on each of the controls in turn.

We will increase the font size of all three controls.

1 Select the controls.

2 Locate the **Appearance** set in the Properties window. The third item down is labelled **Font** and has a ⊞ icon by the side. Click on this to open up the **Font** sub-set.

3 Click into the **Size** field and change the value to 10 – or higher if you prefer. The font size of all the controls will be increased.

4 Click onto a blank area of the form to deselect the controls.

2.5 Setting colours

Colours can be set by typing in colour names or their numeric definitions, but it is ridiculously hard work to try to remember them. The far simpler way is to select them from a palette. The choice is infinite – you have three different palettes to choose from, and you can define your own if nothing else suits.

The three palettes are:

• **System,** which contains the colours that are used by Windows for different screen elements. If you use these colours, when the program is run on a PC with a different colour scheme, your colours will change to match the appropriate element of that scheme.

• The **Web** colours are those which are recognized by HTML and can be displayed by browsers. If you are developing a Web application, you should restrict yourself to this set.

• **Custom** is the most flexible. It has a set of 48 predefined colours, and another 16 which you can define for yourself.

To set a predefined colour:

1 Select a control, then click on one of its colour properties. An arrow will appear on the right of the field.

2 Click the down arrow to open the colour palette.

3 Click on the **Custom, Web** or **System** label to open its tab.

4 Scroll through the list, if necessary, and click on a colour. Set the colours of the controls in the example, as you please.

To define your own colours:

1 Select a control, then click on the colour property to be set.

2 Click the down arrow to open the colour palette.

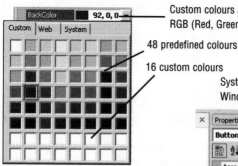

Custom colours are labelled with their RGB (Red, Green, Blue) values

48 predefined colours

16 custom colours

System colours use the Windows colour scheme names

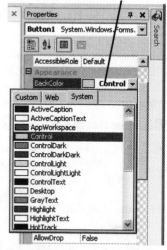

You should use Web colours for Web applications, but they can also be used for any others – you have 128 colours to choose from

Use System colours if you want your colours to match the Windows colour scheme on whatever PC the program is run.

Figure 2.5 The colour palettes.

3 Click on the **Custom** label to open its tab.

4 Right-click on one of the empty boxes at the bottom.

5 At the **Define Color** dialog box, drag the cross over the main rainbow display to set the basic colour, then drag the slider up or down the scale on the right to set its brightness.

6 Click **Add Color**.

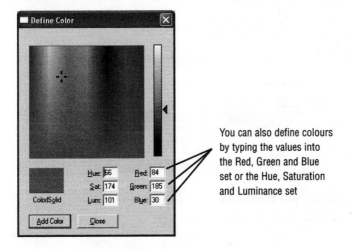

You can also define colours by typing the values into the Red, Green and Blue set or the Hue, Saturation and Luminance set

You will find one (simple) example of setting colours during the program's run in section 3.7, and more in Chapter 9.

2.6 Formatting text

We have already set the size of text. Let's turn now to the other Font properties. These can all be set in one operation through the Font dialog box, or individually in their fields in the Property window. The Font properties are: Name, Size, Unit, Bold, GdiCharSet, GdiVerticalFont, Italic, Strikeout and Underline.

• To set the **Name**, select it from the list – the choice depends upon what fonts are installed in your PC.

• To set the **Size**, type a value. This is normally given in points, but you can set the **Units** to pixels, inches, millimetres or other more specialist units of measure if you prefer.

* **Bold, Italic, Strikeout** and **Underline** are True/False values – drop down the list and select to turn the effect on or off.

* **GdiCharSet** and **GdiVerticalFont** refer to the GDI (graphical design interface) system which gives you more flexible ways of rendering fonts. Read up on this in the Help system if you are interested – it is too specialist a topic for this short book.

To set Font properties:

1 Select the control(s).

Either

2 Click on the **Font** line [Font   **Arial, 16pt**] then click the ▒.

3 At the **Font** dialog box, set the font, style, size and other effects, using the **Sample** as a guide, then click **OK**.

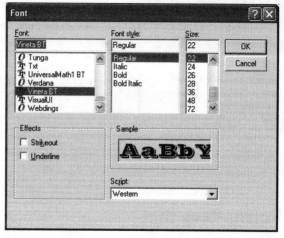

Or

4 Click ⊞ to open the **Font** group, and set individual properties as required.

- Using either method, format the Label text to make it large and loud. The Button and TextBox could be a little more restrained.

Alignment

In Visual Basic, text always exists within a bounded space. This may be the very restricted face of a small button, it may be a window-sized text area, or anything in between. Whatever the size, the space has two dimensions – height and width – and boundaries. Within it, you can align text to the left, centre or right, and also align it vertically to the top, middle or bottom.

To set the alignment:

1 Go to the bottom of the **Appearance** set.

2 Select **TextAlign** and click the down arrow.

3 Click on a button to select the vertical and horizontal alignment.

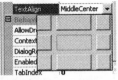

Set the **Label** text to *MiddleCenter* alignment.

Some aspects of setting Font properties at run time are explored briefly in section 3.4, and – more thoroughly – in Chapter 8.

2.7 Programming with properties

Now, let's get back to our project. We want to add code to the *Copy* button to copy the text from the *UserInput* Textbox to the *Output* Label. This line is all that you need:

```
Output.Text = UserInput.Text
```

Output.Text identifies the Text property of the Output control. The = sign is an *assignment* instruction – its value is to be made equal to the value of the *UserInput.Text* property.

Visual Studio is very helpful when you are writing properties into code. When you reach a point where a property is expected, i.e. after you have typed the name of the control and the dot, a list of the control's properties appears. Scroll down through the list, or type the first letter to bring that part of the list into view, then double-click on the property and it will be written into the

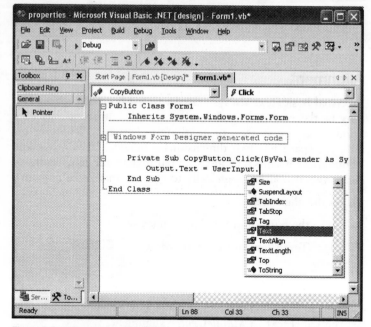

Figure 2.6 When you need to write a property, the list appears.

code for you. With something like *Text*, this is no great help, but you will appreciate it when you want to set the *DefaultBackColor* or find the *ControlAccessibleObject*.

Double-click on the *Copy* button to switch to the code display. The cursor should be in the *CopyButton.Click* sub. Type in the line to assign the text from *UserInput* to *Output*.

Remember that the system will correct the capitalization of the names of controls, properties and other words that it recognizes and use only lower case when typing. When you reach the end of the line, press [**Enter**] to activate the capitalization. If the system does not adjust the capitals of a name, you must have mistyped it.

We are now going to add code to the *Output* label so that it is wiped clear when you click on it. This means that we need to get into the *Output.Click* sub. There are two ways to do this. We could go back to the form display and double-click on *Output*. But we can also do it without leaving the code display.

At the top of the code display are two drop-down lists: on the left, the **Class** list contains the controls and other objects currently present in the project; on the right the **Method** list holds the methods that can be applied to the selected object.

To start a new sub from the code display:

1 Open the **Class** list and select the control, here use *Output*.

2 Open the **Method** list and select the sub, in this case *Click*.

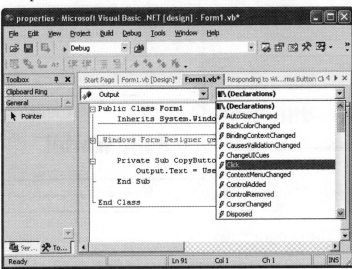

3 The framework for the sub – its header and end sub lines – will be written into the code display. Add the line:

   Output.Text = ""

4 The code is complete. Time to test it!

Public and Private

Note that the class itself (i.e. the program) is marked 'Public' and the Subs are all marked 'Private'. These control whether or not data in the blocks can be accessed from outside.

Does it work?

1 Press [F5] to build and run the program. After a moment you will see the form as a window, with the *UserInput* highlighted.

2 Type in your own text and click the *Copy* button. Is the text copied into the *Output*?

3 Click on the *Output*. Is it cleared?

4 Click the **Close** button to close the window.

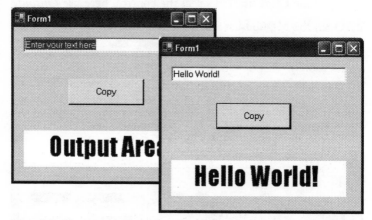

Figure 2.7 The program when it first appears, and after entering and copying text.

The program file

After you have built a project successfully, if you look in its bin folder you will find a file with the project name and an .exe extension. This is a stand-alone Windows program. Double-click on it to run it directly from My Computer.

The program file can run on any PC with the standard Visual Basic runtime files installed – it does not need the development system.

2.8 Tidy exits

Clicking the Close button is one way to end a program, but we really ought to provide a proper exit. It is not difficult – all it takes is a single word in the code, and something to attach it to.

1 Add another button to the form, labelling it 'Exit'.

2 Double-click on it to get into its **Click** sub and type the word:

   End

3 That is all you need. *End* stops anything that may be happening in a program and closes its window.

4 Press [F5] to build and run the program again, and see.

2.9 MsgBox

We have already used the MsgBox to display messages, but there is a lot more to this function. It is such a useful tool for interacting with your users that you should learn how to use it early on.

The basic syntax of the function is:

    ReturnValue = MsgBox("Prompt", StyleCode, "Title")

Much of this is optional. You can pare it down to the minimal MsgBox("Prompt") if you just want to display a message with an OK button.

The style code controls which buttons to display – and there are six different combinations of **OK, Cancel, Yes, No, Abort** and **Retry**. It also controls which, if any, of the four possible icons to include – ⊗, ❓, ⚠, ⓘ. These can be specified using keywords or numeric codes, though the keywords only allow you to specify the buttons or the icon – not both at once.

Keyword	Code	Result
OKOnly	0	OK button only
OKCancel	1	OK and Cancel buttons
AbortRetryIgnore	2	Abort, Retry and Ignore buttons
YesNoCancel	3	Yes, No and Cancel buttons
YesNo	4	Yes and No buttons
RetryCancel	5	Retry and Cancel buttons
Critical	16	Critical message icon ⊗
Question	32	Warning query icon ❓
Exclamation	48	Warning message icon ⚠
Information	64	Information message icon ⓘ

Examples

Explore the MsgBox buttons and icons with these examples. Type them into the Form_Load sub – double-click on the background of any form to get into code and open this sub.

When you type a comma after the prompt, the list of MsgBoxStyle options will appear. Double-click on an option in the list to write it into the code.

Yes and No buttons

```
MsgBox("Are you sure you want to do _
this?", MsgBoxStyle.YesNo, "YesNo")
```

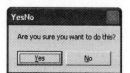

OK and Cancel buttons

```
MsgBox("Do you really want to quit?", _
MsgBoxStyle.OKCancel, "OKCancel")
```

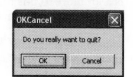

Query icon

As we have not specified the buttons, the simple OK button is displayed.

```
MsgBox("Do you really want to quit?", _
MsgBoxStyle.Question, "Question")
```

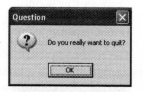

Critical message icon

```
MsgBox("This is a really bad idea!", _
MsgBoxStyle.Critical, "Critical")
```

Long lines of code

Where a line of code is too long to fit across the page, an underline _ at the end of the line indicates that it continues on to the next. Write these joined lines as one continuous line of code. For example, if you see this:

```
MsgBox("Are you sure?", MsgBoxStyle.YesNo, _
"YesNo")
```

you should write this:

```
MsgBox("Are you sure?", MsgBoxStyle.YesNo,  "YesNo")
```

OK and Cancel buttons with a Query

Instead of two keywords, we take the codes (32 = warning query and 1 = OKCancel), add them together and write in the result.

```
MsgBox("Do you really want to _
quit?",33,"Style code 32 + 1 = 33")
```

Warning message icon

```
MsgBox("Danger! Danger!", MsgBoxStyle. _
Exclamation, "Exclamation")
```

Abort, Retry and Ignore buttons

```
MsgBox("There is no disk in the drive", MsgBoxStyle. _
AbortRetryIgnore, "AbortRetryIgnore")
```

Abort, Retry and Ignore buttons with a Warning message icon

And again, to get both buttons and an icon we use the numeric codes: 48 (warning message) and 2 (AbortRetryIgnore).

```
MsgBox("There is no disk in the drive",50,"Style code 48 + 2 = 50")
```

Return values

If you want anything more than an OK button, you need to know what the user clicked. Though MsgBox() can be used as a simple *statement* – code which performs an action of some sort – it is actually a *function* – a block of code which produces a value.

```
Response = MsgBox("Do you want to go on?", MsgBoxStyle.YesNo)
```

In this line, the user's choice of button is fed back into the program through the variable *Response*. (A *variable* is a named place in memory where values can be stored. We will look at them properly in Chapter 4.)

The values returned by the different buttons are listed here.

Button	Value
OK	1
Cancel	2
Abort	3
Retry	4
Ignore	5
Yes	6
No	7

Here's a simple example of how return values can be used to control the actions of a program.

```
Check = MsgBox("Really quit?", 33, "Exit check")
If (Check = 6) Then End
```

You'll see some more fully worked examples later, when we have covered rather more of the basics.

Methods, subs and functions

There are two types of methods in Visual Basic. A subroutine (or sub) is a self-contained block of code that performs a task. A function is also a self-contained block of code, but one which produces a value – numeric, text or other. We will explore their similarities and differences in Chapter 6.

2.10 InputBox

The InputBox function uses a ready-made Windows dialog box to collect inputs from the user. The syntax is:

```
Variable = InputBox("Prompt", "Title", "Default value, Xpos,Ypos)
```

Only the *Variable* and the *Prompt* are essential. The *Title* will be written into the title bar; the *Xpos* and *Ypos* set the distance (in pixels) of the top left corner of the box from the top left corner of the screen. If the *Xpos* and *Ypos* are omitted, the InputBox will by placed centrally, one third of the way down the screen.

```
UserName = InputBox("Please enter your name", "User name entry")
```

This produces the following display.

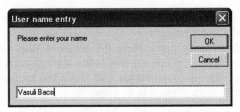

If the user presses [Enter] or clicks OK, the value in the InputBox will be stored in the variable *UserName*. If Cancel is clicked, the input is not copied to the variable.

InputBoxes are useful for collecting essential information as all other program activity is suspended until the user has responded.

You will see examples of the InputBox in use when we explore variables and program flow in Chapters 4 and 5.

2.11 Comments

One of the major problems faced by programmers is remembering how their programs worked when they return to them after a few months. And trying to make sense of another person's code can be a nightmare.

There are two main ways in which you can make your programs more readable and easier for you and others to understand. The first is to give meaningful names to all your objects, variables (see Chapter 4), subroutines and functions (see Chapter 6). The second is to write comments to explain what things do and why.

A comment is marked by a single apostrophe at the start. It can be written after the code on the same line, or as a separate line by itself.

```
Output.Text = Result        'display the result of the calculation
...
repeat = InputBox("How many times?")
' ask the user how many times to repeat the operation
```

Visual Studio will recolour the comments in green so that they stand out, and the compiler will ignore everything after the apostrophe when it is building the code into a program.

> ## 'Commenting out'
>
> **When you are developing a program it is sometimes useful to take code temporarily out of play so that you can concentrate on a particularly troublesome section of the program. Typing an apostrophe at the start of each line will turn the code into comments and make the compiler skip over those lines when it is building the program.**

Exercises

1 Set up a form with three Labels and three TextBoxes, side by side. The TextBoxes should be named UserName, Address and Email, as they will hold these details. Type suitable text for the labels. Add a Button, with the text "Get details".

Explore the Properties for the controls and experiment with those that affect the appearance – but not the behaviour.

Write code in the Button's Click event handler that will use InputBoxes to collect the three items of data and copy them into the TextBoxes.

2 Switch the lights on and off! Set up a form with a Label and two Buttons. Set these properties:

Form   BackColor = white

Label   BackColor = white; ForeColor = black

Button1 Text = 'On'; Enabled = False

Button2 Text = 'Off'

Write code on the Off button to change both BackColors to black, enable the On button and disable the Off button.

Write code on the On button to reverse the same settings.

If your programs don't work, compare your code with that given in Chapter 12, *Answers to exercises*.

Summary

- ◆ Visual Basic is an object-oriented language. Objects have properties and methods which control their appearance, behaviour and interaction with other objects.

- ◆ The user-interface is created by locating and defining controls, in the Design window.

- ◆ Code is typed and edited in the Code window.

- ◆ The properties of controls can be set at design time by setting options or typing values in the Properties window.

- ◆ Colours can be selected from the Custom, Web or System palettes.

- ◆ Each aspect of a font can be set individually, or the whole format can be defined in the Font dialog box.

- ◆ Properties can be set from the code – this is how you change the screen while the program is running.

- ◆ The MsgBox function provides a simple and efficient way to communicate with the user.

- ◆ An InputBox can be used to collect data from a user.

- ◆ Comments should be added freely to make your code more readable.

03

controls and events

In this chapter you will learn:

- about mouse events and how to trap them
- how to collect data through different types of controls
- how to pick up keypresses
- about the focus and tab order

3.1 Mouse events

An event is an action which affects an object in some way. There are several dozen different types of events, though not all can happen to every object. For example, any visible object can be clicked on, but only TextBoxes can have their text changed.

Let's start by looking at mouse events. We have already met the most-used one – Click. Other common mouse events are:

* **MouseDown:** the left button is pushed down.

* **MouseUp:** the left button is released.

* **MouseEnter:** the pointer is somewhere over the object.

* **MouseLeave:** the pointer has moved away.

You need a little care when using **MouseDown** and **MouseUp** at the same time as **Click**, because when the user starts to click, the initial press will be picked up by **MouseDown** not by **Click**.

Start a new project and create a form like the one in Figure 3.1. It should have a PictureBox, a Label and a Button.

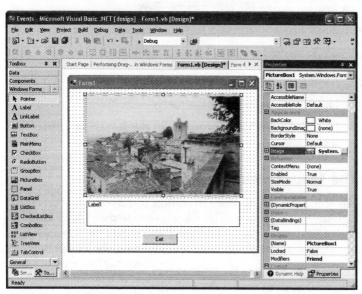

Figure 3.1 A form with a PictureBox, Label and Button for testing mouse events. You don't have to use a PictureBox, but it does give you the chance to explore that control.

Change the **Name** of the Label to *Caption*, and change the Button's **Text** property to read '*Exit*'.

Images and the PictureBox

Visual Basic can handle image files in the main bitmap and metafile formats: BMP, JPG, JPEG, GIF, PNG, ICO, EMF and WMF. By default, images are displayed at their original size, which may well be smaller or larger than the PictureBox, and located at the top left of the PictureBox. The **SizeMode** property offers four ways of fitting the image to the PictureBox:

◆ **Normal** is the default.

◆ **StretchImage** shrinks or expands the picture to fit, and will distort it if the image and the PictureBox are different shapes.

◆ **AutoSize** makes the box adjust to the size of the picture.

◆ **CentreImage** aligns the centres of the image and the PictureBox so that there are equal margins around the image, or an even amount is trimmed off all round.

To load an image file into a PictureBox:

1 Place a new PictureBox or select an existing one.

2 Click on the **Image** property to highlight it.

3 Click the ⬚ button to open the **Open** dialog box.

4 Locate and open the image file.

5 Locate the **SizeMode** property, in the **Behaviour** group, and set an appropriate option.

The Mouse event code

We will add code to the PictureBox to respond to any mouse activity that affects it. The **Click** event is the default method, and we can open the code display and create the framework of its subroutine simply by double-clicking on the PictureBox.

To write the code for the other events, we will have to start their subroutines from within the code display.

1 Double-click on the PictureBox.

2 In Sub **Click**, write the line:

```
Caption.Text = "You clicked on the pic"
```

3 Drop down the **Method** list at the top right of the Code window and select **MouseDown**.

4 When its Sub code appears, write in this line:

```
Caption.Text = "The mouse is down"
```

5 Repeat steps **3** and **4** to add the following code to handle the **MouseUp, MouseEnter** and **MouseLeave** events. (To keep the code display clearer, I've omitted the parameters on the Sub lines – just leave them as they are.)

```
Private Sub PictureBox1_MouseUp(...
    Caption.Text = "The mouse is up"
End Sub

Private Sub PictureBox1_MouseEnter(...
    Caption.Text = "The mouse is over the picture"
End Sub

Private Sub PictureBox1_MouseLeave(...
    Caption.Text = "The mouse has left the picture"
End Sub
```

6 Select the button from the **Class** list at the top left of the Code window, and Click from the **Method** list. Write the **End** keyword into Sub **Click** so that it will end the program.

7 Press [F5] to build and run the program.

♦ If you get a 'Build error' report, go back into the code and check the spelling and punctuation – have you enclosed all the Caption.Text in double quotes?

Test the program's response to mouse events. Move over and off the picture. Click on it. Hold the mouse down and release after a moment. What do you notice?

You should have found that the Click code does not seem to work. When you click, you only appear to get the MouseDown and MouseUp messages. Is the Click message overwritten too quickly for us to see, or is the Click event ignored completely?

Let's test. Go back into the code and add this line into Sub Click:

```
MsgBox("You clicked")
```

This will generate a MessageBox, which will stay on screen until you clear it by clicking its OK button. If it does not appear, that will tell you that the Click event has not been triggered.

Build and run the project again, then click on the picture. What happens?

Figure 3.2 Testing mouse events. Here, the pointer has moved over the picture area, triggering the MouseEnter event.

Test programs

Try to test out every new idea as you read. Place the control, set the properties (and explore those that aren't covered here), type in the code and run the resulting program.

Testing is best done on a clean form, so that you can focus on the new idea, but starting a new project every time will steadily clutter up your projects folder. Instead of starting a new project, clear the form and reuse the same one. When you get into the Code window, the first job you should do is delete the subs left over from the previous test. A sub is not deleted when its control is removed from the form.

3.2 Values and ScrollBars

There are a several ways that users can set values in programs. Here we will look at the events of the controls of the ScrollBar family. There are four closely related controls: HScrollBar, VScrollBar, TrackBar and NumericUpDown.

HScrollBar and VScrollBar

The horizontal and vertical scrollbars are identical in use, with the sole exception of their orientation.

They have a **Value** property which is changed when the slider is moved. It can be moved in three ways: by clicking on the bar above or below the slider; by clicking on the arrows at the ends; by dragging the slider. Whichever way is used, it triggers the same **Scroll** event – which makes life easier for the programmer.

There are four other properties which determine the range of values, and the amount by which they change when the user clicks on the scrollbar.

- **Minimum** sets the lowest value – the default is 0

- **Maximum** sets the highest value – the default is 100

- **LargeChange** sets the amount the value changes when the user clicks on the bar beside the slider – the default is 10

- **SmallChange** sets the amount the value changes when the user clicks on the arrow at the end – the default is 1

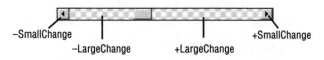

ScrollBars can be placed anywhere on a form and be any size. They have a **Docked** property which can be set to *Top*, *Bottom*, *Left*, *Right*, *Fill* (I haven't found a use for that one yet!) or *None*.

ScrollBars are convenient for setting approximate values – and you will notice that there is no scale on them. If you want to display the value of a ScrollBar, you need to copy it into a Label or TextBox.

1 Place a **Label** on a form.

2 Name the Label, *ScrollDisplay*.

3 Place an **HScrollBar** on the form and name it *Scroller*.

4 Double-click on the *Scroller* to display the code. It should open with the cursor in Sub Scroller_Scroll( ). Write this line:

```
ScrollDisplay.Text = Scroller.Value
```

5 Press [F5] to build and run the program.

Click on the scrollbar and on its arrows, and drag the slider. Watch the display. What is the highest you can get it?

Close the program and back at the Form Design display, set the Maximum to 1000 and the LargeChange to 100. Run the program again and test it. What is the highest possible value now?

For reasons best known to Microsoft, the highest value that a user can get on a ScrollBar is Maximum – LargeChange + 1.

TrackBar

This variation on the scrollbar theme has only two ways to move the slider – by dragging it or by clicking on the bar (LargeChange). As there are no end arrows, there is no SmallChange property.

The TrackBar has a scale, with 10 ticks by default, and the slider moves in discrete hops from one tick to another, instead of the smooth continuous change of a ScrollBar. The number of ticks is the difference between the Maximum and Minimum properties.

If you need to display the value of a TrackBar, you can copy it into a Label or TextBox, by adding code to its Scroll event – in exactly the same way as we did with the HScrollBar.

```
TrackDisplay.Text = Tracker.Value
```

Alternatively, you could add Labels, bearing the appropriate values, at the ends of the TrackBar or beneath the ticks.

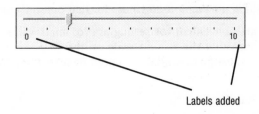

Labels added

TrackBars have the same **Docked** options as HScrollBars, but are less flexible in their sizing. A TrackBar can be any length you like, but you cannot change its depth.

NumericUpDown

This control is, in effect, a TextBox with a squashed VScrollBar on the side. Values can be typed directly into the display area, or changed by clicking the up/down arrows. These adjust the value by the amount of the **Increment** property (the equivalent of **SmallChange** on ScrollBars).

If a program needs to respond to a change in the value, write code into the **ValueChanged** event.

The height of a NumericUpDown is set by the font size – the default is 8.25 point text, giving a 20 pixel high control. The width can be set to anything you want, but should be at least wide enough to display the maximum value.

3.3 Text controls

There are four controls which can display text. They share some properties, e.g. Font and BorderStyle, but they have their own special properties and possibilities. We have already met two of them in passing. Let's take a closer look at them and meet the other two text controls.

Label

The Label is purely for display and cannot be edited by the user. Use it for headings, titles and other identifying or descriptive text. The label can be any width or depth, with text wrapping round a second or further lines if necessary. Text can be aligned both vertically and horizontally – unlike TextBoxes where only horizontal alignment is possible.

You can also display an image in a Label, but it must be the right size before you import it as there is no SizeMode property here (unlike the PictureBox, see page 47). This is probably best used for icons to accompany the text.

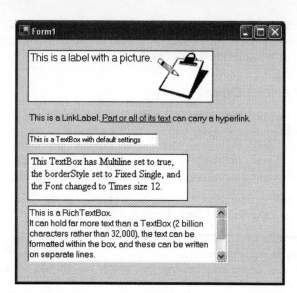

Figure 3.3 Text controls – notice the vertical scrollbar on the RichTextBox. This is a default setting. Horizontal and/or vertical scrollbars can be shown on any TextBox.

LinkLabel

A LinkLabel is the same as an ordinary Label except for one thing – part or all of its text can be made into a hyperlink. The target for the hyperlink is not written into the properties – so this is not as simple to set up as a hyperlink in a web page editor or even in Word. Instead, the jump to the target page or file is written into the code of the **LinkClicked** event which is activated when the user clicks on the link.

To hyperlink one part of the text:

1 Click ⊡ to open the **LinkArea** properties and enter the **Start** character and the **Length** of the string to link.

Or

2 Click the ⊞ beside **LinkArea** to open the **LinkArea Editor**.

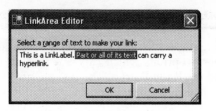

3 Highlight the text to link and click **OK**.

TextBox

We have already seen how a TextBox can display text and collect text inputs. So far we have only used them for small quantites of text, but these boxes can take up to 32,000 characters. How can it fit? There are two properties that enable larger quantities of text to fit – and to be seen.

• **Multiline**, in the Behaviour group, is set to *False* by default, producing a single-line box. Set this to *True* if you want to be able to deepen the box.

• **Scrollbars**, in the Appearance group, can be set to *None*, *Horizontal*, *Vertical* or *Both*. When the program runs, if either or both scrollbars are turned on, they will be greyed out if the text fits within the box, but will become active if the text expands.

Unlike Labels, TextBoxes cannot take images.

RichTextBox

This has all the features of the standard TextBox, and more. For a start it can hold far more – up to 2 billion characters! It can also take fully formatted text, i.e. with different fonts, alignments and other settings applied to different sections, and the text can have embedded graphics or data. At design time you can only set the font for the whole box, but within the program you can have code to select and reformat any size block of text, and the user can paste in any formatted text. In Chapters 8 and 9, you will see a RichTextBox in use when we create our own word processor.

The default settings for a RichTextBox produce a Multiline box with a vertical scrollbar.

3.4 Toggle switches

In Visual Basic, as elsewhere in Windows, you find two kinds of toggle switches – options which can be either on or off – the CheckBox and the RadioButton. The two are used similarly but with one very real difference.

CheckBox

Every CheckBox is an independent option – whether one is on or off should not have any effect on any other CheckBox. Text can be formatted with any combination of bold, italic, underline or strikethrough effects – it may look awful if you use them all at once, but it's possible.

The key property of a CheckBox is *Checked* – which is True or False depending upon whether or not it is ticked – and its most useful method is *CheckedChanged* which is triggered by a click on the box.

For example, a word processing program might have a CheckBox called *BoldBox*. The code to test its status might start:

```
Private Sub BoldBox_CheckedChanged(...
    If BoldBox.Checked = True Then
    ...
```

'= True' can be omitted, so that the second line could be written more briefly, but with exactly the same effect, like this:

```
If BoldBox.Checked Then...
```

We will deal with the If … Then structure in Chapter 5.

Figure 3.4 A person may have visited several continents – but see the next example.

RadioButton

RadioButtons are designed to work in sets. If one RadioButton in a set is switched on, then the rest will automatically be switched off. Use them to set options where choices are mutually exclusive, for example, text cannot be aligned to the left and centre at the same time.

A RadioButton has a *Checked* property and a *CheckedChanged* method which are used in exactly the same way as those of a CheckBox.

Figure 3.5 There can only be one continent which you call home, so for this we need to use RadioButtons.

GroupBox

The GroupBox is simply a container – put any selection of controls in one and you can then move, format, copy or otherwise work with the whole lot in a single operation. However, they also serve a special function with RadioButtons. Put a set of buttons in a GroupBox and it will keep them independent of any other RadioButtons elsewhere on the form. So, if you need two sets of RadioButtons on a form, put one – or both – sets in thier own GroupBox.

If you find that you need to use a GroupBox after you have created a set of RadioButtons (or any other objects), this is not a problem. Simply place a new GroupBox on the form, then drag the objects across and drop them into it.

Figure 3.6 You can have several sets of RadioButtons on a form, but you must enclose each set in a GroupBox.

3.5 Keyboard events

The TextBox, and those controls that have a text entry component, have a TextChanged event. This is activated by typing into the control. Try this to see it in action.

1 Place a **Label** and a **TextBox** on a form, naming them *Display* and *TextInput*.

2 Double-click on the TextBox. The Code window will open at the **TextChanged** sub. Write in this line:

```
Display.Text = TextInput.Text
```

3 Press [F5] to build and run the program.

You should find that as text is entered or edited in the TextBox, it is echoed in the Label.

Capturing keypresses

If you want to be able to pick up keypresses at any point during a program, rather than just when a text box is active, you can use the **OnKeyPress()** method. This is one from a *base* class and not linked to any control – you will find them under the heading **Overrides** in the Class list. These methods can be redefined, or *overridden*. Overriding only really becomes significant with more complex programs where you are using **Inherits** to pass definitions of classes from one block of code to another. It is worth knowing about at this level because the overridable methods include some very useful ones for interacting with the system.

Test it. This little routine will pick up keypresses and tell you the character and ASCII code of the pressed key. Note that neither the function nor the movement keys are recognized by this.

```
Protected Overrides Sub OnKeyPress(By Val e As System.Windows. _
Forms.KeyPressEventArgs)
    Dim key As Char = e.KeyChar
    MsgBox("Character = " & key & " ASCII code = " & Asc(key)
End Sub
```

The Dim line creates a variable called *key* which holds the **KeyChar** property (the character) of the *e* argument – this picks up the keypress from the system. **Asc()** gives the ASCII code. This line will make more sense after you have read about variables (Chapter 4) and arguments (section 6.2).

3.6 The Focus

In any Windows form or dialog box, at any given time, one control will have the 'focus'. You can normally tell which has the focus simply by looking – it is the TextBox containing the highlighted text or flashing cursor, the Button with the double outline. It is the one where text will appear if you type, or which will be actioned if you press [Enter]. If a program has multiple windows, the active one has the focus.

The user can change the focus by pressing [Tab] or by clicking onto the control or the window. Changes of focus are picked up by the events GotFocus and LostFocus. These can apply to any control, and also to forms. We will see these in action in a moment, but first let's look at how the focus moves around a form.

3.7 TabIndex

The **TabIndex** sets the order in which pressing [Tab] moves the focus from one control to the next. Initially a control's TabIndex is the same as the order in which it was placed on the form at design time, but this will not necessarily be the best order that you want. This is not a problem as the TabIndex can be changed.

Try this example. It produces a form with three TextBoxes with coloured text. When a box has the focus, the text will change to black, reverting to its previous colour when the focus moves on.

1 Set up a form containing three TextBoxes and a Button.

2 Name the TextBoxes *Box1*, *Box2* and *Box3*.

3 Use the Web palette and change their ForeColor settings to *Red*, *Green* and *Blue*.

4 Label the Button 'Exit'.

5 Select *Box1*, and set its **TabIndex** property (in the Behaviour group) to 1.

6 Set the **TabIndex** of *Box2* to 2, *Box3* to 3 and of the exit Button to 4.

◆ *Always check the TabIndex order! The system does not check this, so you can have two or more controls with the same TabIndex, which can produce unexpected effects at run-time.*

7 Double-click on Box1 to open the Code window. The cursor will be in its TextChange sub. We will not be using this. Drop down the Method list and select GotFocus.

Write in this line:

```
Box1.ForeColor = Color.Black
```

Note how the colour is specified. Fortunately it is not necessary to remember the colour names. After you have typed the **Color.** keyword and the dot, a list of colour names will appear – simply select from there.

8 Add code to change the colour back to red when the focus moves to the next control. Select LostFocus from the Method list and write this line:

```
Box1.ForeColor = Color.Red
```

9 Add similar code to Box2 and Box3, changing the ForeColor to black when they get the focus, then reverting to their original colours when they lose the focus.

10 Add code to the Button to end the program.

11 Build and run the program.

12 Tab between the TextBoxes to check the order. As the text is automatically highlighted when a TextBox gets the focus, the colour change will not be immediately obvious. Type something and you will see that the text is now black.

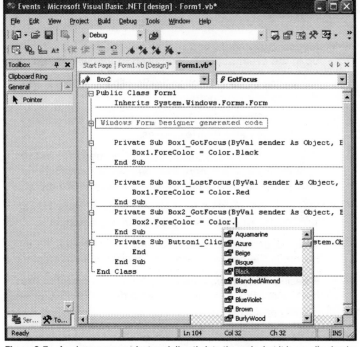

Figure 3.7 A colour name can be typed directly into the code, but it is usually simpler to select it from the list that appears when you use the Color keyword.

Exercises

1 Set up a form around 500×500. Place a VScrollBar the length of one side and an HScrollBar across the bottom, setting the range of both at 0–500. Place a small PictureBox at the top left of the form. Link the Left and Top properties of the PictureBox to the scrollbars so that they control its position.

2 A firm needs to know which Office applications its staff can use. Create a data entry form for a survey. It should have TextBoxes for the name, workgroup and contact number, and CheckBoxes or RadioButtons (as appropriate) for sex, age group and the applications which the respondent can use. Check that the form can be used as required. Save the project – we will build on this form in later exercises.

Summary

- ◆ Mouse movements and mouse actions can be picked up in the event handlers, and used to trigger routines.

- ◆ Values can be given through the Scrollbars, Trackbar and NumericUpDown controls.

- ◆ Text can be displayed in Labels, or displayed and entered in TextBoxes and RichTextBoxes.

- ◆ CheckBoxes and RadioButtons can be used for on/off options. If you have more than one set of RadioButtons on a form, you must enclose each later set in a GroupBox.

- ◆ You can pick up the event when the user types into a TextBox, or when a key is pressed in any situation.

- ◆ When a control comes into and out of focus – i.e. becomes the active control – an event occurs.

- ◆ Pressing [Tab] moves the focus from one control to the next, according to their TabIndex order.

04

variables and operations

In this chapter you will learn:

- about data types
- how to declare variables and assign values to them
- about constants and arrays
- how to store data in files
- about arithmetic and bitwise operators

4.1 Data types

A variable is a named part of memory in which data is stored. The amount of the memory allocated to a variable depends upon its type – you obviously need far less space to store a small whole number than you do a large value with lots of decimal places, and this will take less space than a pageful of text.

Visual Basic uses these variable types:

Type	Bytes	Data stored
Short	2	Whole numbers in the range –32,767 to +32,767
Integer	4	Whole numbers in the range –2,147,483,647 to +2,147,483,647
Long	8	Whole numbers in the range +/– 9 billion billion
Single	4	Floating point (decimal) values in the range +/–3.4^38, accurate to 8 significant figures
Double	8	Floating point values in the range +/–1.8^108, accurate to 18 significant figures
Decimal	16	Decimal values accurate to 29 significant figures
Byte	1	Character or integer in the range 0 to 255
Char	2	Character, using the Unicode set
String	N/A	Block of text, of up to 65,000 characters
Date	8	Date value, held as a number, counting in units of 100 nanoseconds, starting from 1st January 0001. The date is entered and displayed in a standard format, e.g. 7/11/2003 9:30 AM
Object	N/A	OLE objects – imported data structure
Boolean	1	1 or 0 = True or False

You can also define your own variable types and declare any kind of object as a variable.

When setting up number variables, think about the size of numbers that will be stored in them, and the accuracy to which they must be held, then select the smallest type that will do the job. There is no point in using a Long, or worse a Decimal, variable to store whole numbers in the range 1 to 1000. A Short is enough and will use less memory and be processed faster.

Visual Basic allows you to perform calculations using different types of number variables. The values will normally be converted up to match the largest type in the expression. We will return to this shortly.

4.2 Declaring variables

A variable must be *declared* before it can be used. This allocates the space in memory and links it to the name. Declaration is done using the **Dim** keyword in this form:

    Dim varName As varType

The *varName* can be any acceptable name (see the boxed item below). The *varType* is the type name, as in the table opposite. Some examples:

    Dim userAge As Short

This will hold the age in whole years.

    Dim myWage As Single

As the wage may have a decimal component (the pence), we need to use a floating point type, but 8 significant figures will be enough – it could accurately hold values up to 999,999.99.

    Dim bossWage As Decimal

Rules for variable names
Variable names:

* may contain any letters or numbers;
* must not use any punctuation symbols except for the under_score;
* must not exceed 255 characters in length.

And you will make life much easier for yourself if you make the names meaningful, and keep them short – anything over 32 characters is too long to read comfortably.

If the name is a combination of two or more words, start each word with a capital to make it easier to read, e.g. MyAge, FinalSalary, CostOfLivingIncrease.

You can use a Visual Basic keyword as a name, but you must then enclose it in [square brackets], or precede it with the name of the form, e.g. [Next] or myForm.Next. It is probably better to simply avoid the keywords.

The boss's wage may well be too much for a Single. A Double could hold up to 9,999,999,999,999,999.99, but we may as well use a Decimal just in case this boss is a bit greedier than average.

```
Dim keypress As Char
```

We can use a Char to hold a single character.

```
Dim userName As String
```

A String variable can take any length of text. If you need to know the length, it is easily found – see Chapter 9.

4.3 Assigning values to variables

Values are assigned to variables using the '=' equals sign, in statements like this:

```
Variable = value or expression producing a value
```

At the simplest, the value is given directly:

```
userAge = 32
```

If the value is text, it must be enclosed in double quotes:

```
ErrorMessage = "Please enter a number between 1 and 10"

keypress = "X"
```

The value may be produced by a function:

```
userName = InputBox("Please enter your name")
```

Or the value can be the result of a calculation, and this may include variables or literal values:

```
Total = 2 + 3 + 4 + 5

VATamount = Total * .175

Count = Count + 1
```

Notice in the last example that the same variable appears on both sides. When the system reaches this line, it will look up the current value in *Count*, add 1 to it, and assign the new variable back to *Count*.

Boolean variables can be assigned the values *True* or *False* – notice that there are no quotes round these words as they are constants (see 4.5). However, they will typically take their value from a logical test, as they are mainly used to carry the results of tests from one part of the program to another.

```
Overdrawn = False
Overdrawn = Cheque > Balance
    ...
If Overdrawn Then...
```

Here we have a Boolean variable, *Overdrawn*. This is set to False at the start, but will be set to True if *Cheque* is greater than *Balance*. Later, the program will take a course of action if only Overdrawn is True. You will see examples of Boolean variables in action in Chapter 5.

Dates are assigned values using the format:

```
#m/d/yyyy h:min:sec AM/PM#
```

That is, the date is entered in numbers, month first, and the year given in four digits. The time is given in 24-hour clock values, or 12-hour clock if AM or PM is specified afterwards. The date or the time can be given by themselves; the seconds can be omitted. The values must be enclosed in #hashes#.

Some examples of valid date assignments:

```
myBirthday = #4/5/1965#
```

i.e. April 5th, and I'm lying about my age.

```
startTime = #14:30#
```

i.e. 2.30 in the afternoon – and the syntax checker will automatically convert this to #2:30:00 PM#.

```
thisMomentNow = #12/20/2003 1:35 PM#
```

i.e. it's just after 1.30 in the afternoon of 20th December 2003.

How dates and times are normally displayed depends upon the settings in the Regional Options in Windows.

The **DateTimePicker** and **MonthCalendar** controls offer easy ways to get date inputs from your users.

Worked examples

Write the following blocks of code into Sub Form_Load – the sub that you get when you double-click on a blank form, and which will run when the program first starts. They all follow much the same pattern – one or more variables are declared, values are assigned directly or from the user's entry in an InputBox, then the values are displayed in a MsgBox.

Joining strings with +

A MsgBox displays a single string, but the messages are a combination of literal text and variables. To concatenate them (join them into one string) we use '+' or '&' signs.

Text strings

When joining strings – either literal strings (text in quotes) or variables – you may need to put in extra spaces between them to stop them running into one another.

```
Private Sub Form1_Load(ByVal sender As System.Object, ByVal _
e As System.EventArgs) Handles MyBase.Load
    Dim Person, Letters As String
    Person = InputBox("Name please")
    Letters = InputBox("Enter your qualifications and medals")
    MsgBox("Good day " & Person & " " & Letters)
    End
End Sub
```

The program should produce a messagebox like this – though your qualifications may not be as impressive as J.J.'s.

We could equally well have used '+' signs to join the message string. Change the line to look like this and run it again.

```
MsgBox("Good day " + Person + " " + Letters)
```

Numbers in strings

If you want to join numbers or numeric variables into strings, it is simplest to use the '&'.

```
MsgBox("The total cost will be " & CostPlusVAT)
```

Strictly speaking, '&' is only supposed to work with strings, so you should really convert the number to a string – the **Str()** function will do this for you – but Visual Basic will normally do the conversion for you without being asked.

The '+' sign raises problems as it is also used to add numbers in arithmetic operations (see section 4.8). If you simply wrote **MsgBox("The total is " + c)**, the system would not know if the '+' sign was there to add numbers or to join text. If you use the '+' sign, you must also use **Str()** to convert the number to a string. This will work:

```
MsgBox("The total is " + Str(c))
```

This example uses Integer variables – try it with Short and Long as well, using a range of positive and negative numbers.

```
Dim a, b, c As Integer
a = 99
b = InputBox("Enter a number")
c = a + b
MsgBox("The total is " & c)
```

Once you have typed in the code for the Integer variables, you can easily adapt it for the next.

Decimal variables – experiment with Single and Double as well.

```
Dim a, b, c As Single
a = 123.456
b = InputBox("Enter a decimal number")
c = a + b
MsgBox("The total is " & c)
```

4.4 The scope of variables

Variables can be declared at various places in a project, and where they are declared determines how they can be used.

Variables can be declared at *module* level – on a form, this means in the **Declarations** area at the top of the code, outside of all the methods. These variables can be accessed by any of the code, anywhere in the module, so that a value assigned in one method can be read into another. This is not necessarily the best way to transfer data between methods – we will explore other and better ways in Chapter 6.

A variable can also be declared inside a method. It is then *local*, and values can only be assigned to it and read from it by code within the method. More than that, the variable normally only exists while the method is running. When the program exits from a method, the memory allocated to its variables is released and can then be reused. This is a good thing. If memory was tied up until the end of the program, then you could start to run out of space in a large, active program that handled a lot of data. If necessary, you can insist that a variable is retained by declaring it *Static* – see page 72.

There is a second advantage to using local variables. As each method's set of variables exists separately from those in other methods, it does not matter if the same names are used. There is no danger of accidentally changing the value held in a variable that is needed in another method. You could have a variable called *Num* in half a dozen methods, and each would be totally separate from the rest.

If you have variables with the same name at module and method level, the local variable is the one which is used in the method. The module level variable is only accessed if there is no local variable of the same name. You can see this in the following program, which demonstrates the scope of variables.

For this you will need a form containing two Buttons (and you might also like to add an Exit button to give you a neat exit). Code is added to *Sub Form_Load* and to the buttons' Click subs.

Three variables, X, Y and Z are declared at module level, then some are declared again – X in *Sub Form_Load*, and both X and Z are declared in *Sub Button1_Click*. X, Y and Z are assigned new values in *Sub Form_Load* and in *Sub Button1_Click* – but which X, Y and Z, the module or local variables? The answer can be seen in the single line of code in *Sub Button2_Click* which simply displays the current values in the module variables. You should be able to work out which have been changed, and when.

To declare module level variables:

1 Go into the code display, and select **Declarations** in the **Method** list at the top right.

2 The cursor will be placed at the top of the code. Move it below the line **Inherits System.Windows.Forms.Form**.

3 Type in the following:

```
Dim X, Y, Z As Short
```

To complete the example program:

1 Select *Form1* from the **Class** list on the top left of the Code window, and *Load* from the **Method** list at the top right, then type in this code.

```
Private Sub Form1_Load(ByVal sender As System.Object, ByVal _
e As System.EventArgs) Handles MyBase.Load
    Dim X As Short
    X = 1
    Y = 2
    Z = X + Y
    MsgBox("X = " & X & " Y = " & Y & " Z = " & Z)
End Sub
```

2 Select the code and copy it – you'll see why in a moment.

3 Select *Button1* from the **Class** list and *Click* from the **Method** list. This sub is almost the same as the last – paste in the copied code, then edit the **Dim** line to add the Z variable.

```
Private Sub Button1_Click(ByVal sender As Object, ByVal e As _
System.EventArgs) Handles Button1.Click
    Dim X, Z As Short
    X = 4
    Y = 5
    Z = X + Y
    MsgBox("X = " & X & " Y = " & Y & " Z = " & Z)
End Sub
```

4 Select *Button2* from the **Class** list and *Click* from the **Method** list at the top right. Copy and paste the MsgBox from one of the other subs.

```
Private Sub Button2_Click(ByVal sender As System.Object, _
ByVal e As System.EventArgs) Handles Button2.Click
    MsgBox("X = " & X & " Y = " & Y & " Z = " & Z)
End Sub
```

5 Build and run the program.

Click Button1, then Button2. Note the values displayed by the message boxes at each stage of the program.

You should find that the variables have these values when the program reaches Button2:

X is still 0 – its value when declared, and unchanged by the two subs, both of which had local variables called X;

Y is 5 – the value assigned to it in *Button1_Click*;

Z is 3 – the value assigned in *Form1_Load*, and unchanged by *Button1_Click*, which has its own Z.

Static

A local variable is normally created anew at the start, and thrown away at the end of its method. This would be a problem if you wanted to return to a method several times during a program run and needed to retain the value in a variable from one visit to the next. There is a solution. If you use the **Static** keyword when declaring the variable, the system will keep the variable intact at the end of a method.

Try this example. Write this code into a Button_Click method.

```
Static Dim Count As Short
If (Count = 0) Then Count = 100
MsgBox("Count = " & Count)
Count = Count - 1
```

When you run the program, click the button several times and notice how the value changes. Edit the first line to read:

```
Dim Count As Short
```

Run and test the program again. What's the difference?

4.5 Constants

Variables are so called because the values stored in them can be varied during the execution of the program. *Constants* are also named memory stores, but the values in them do not change – hence the name. The main purpose of using constants is that they can make a program more readable. You have already met some of the constants built into Visual Basic, although they were not pointed out as such at the time. The colour keywords, such as Red, Blue and Green, are constants which provide a simple alternative to the use of complex numbers to define colours.

The Boolean values, True and False, are also constants – they replace the actually values of 1 and 0.

Constants can simplify updating a program at a later date. For example, a program to handle the accounts of a business, would have to do VAT calculations at several different points. If the VAT rate changed, you would need to update the program. If you had used the literal value – 0.175 (17.5%) – you would have to trawl through the program looking for every occurrence of this, and there would be a danger of missing some. If you used a constant, declared at one point in the program, it would only be necesary to make the one change.

Constants are created with the keyword Const, like this:

```
Const VAT = 0.175
```

The scope rules apply to constants the same way as to variables, so declare them where they can be accessed by all those parts of the program that need them.

Try this. It sets up a form with two text boxes – one in which you enter an amount, and one which displays the VAT due on the amount. The VAT is calculated by the line:

```
VATDue.Text = Amount.Text * VAT
```

Think about this line for a moment. It takes a Text property, multiplies it then assigns the new value to a Text property. Strictly speaking, we should convert the string value into a number, perform the calculation on that, then convert the number into a string before assigning it to the Text property. Fortunately, Visual Basic is a forgiving system and will do the conversions for you, without being asked. However, this kind of slack programming does allow errors to creep in. To produce industrial-strength, crash-proof programs, you must do your own conversions – and a lot of other error-trapping as well. For interest, the strictly correct version of that line would be:

```
VATDue.Text = (Val(Amount.Text) * VAT).ToString("F")
```

We will come back to type conversions later.

1 Place two TextBoxes on a form, and name them *Amount* and *VATDue*.

2 Place a button, naming – and labelling – it *Calculate*.

3 In the **Declarations** area at the top of the program, type this:

```
Const VAT = 0.175
```

4 Write this line into Calculate_Click:

```
VATDue.Text = Amount.Text * VAT
```

This will take the value from the Text property of the *Amount* TextBox, multiply it by the VAT rate, and write the result into the *VATDue* TextBox.

5 Build and run the program. Type a simple value – so that you can check the calculation by hand or in your head – into the *Amount* TextBox and click the *Calculate* button. Try some other values, to check that your first, correct, answer wasn't a fluke.

Test values

Every calculation in a program should be tested to make sure that it is doing what you intended. You should test it with three or four sets of input values:

1 Simple values so that you can quickly check that the calculation is accurate.

2 Values of the expected type and within the expected range, e.g. whole numbers between 0 and 100.

3 Values outside the expected range and type, to see how it deals with them, e.g. fractional or negative numbers.

4 If there are definite limits, test the values on the limits, e.g. if values must be between 1 and 6 (inclusive), what happens if you enter 1 or 6. This checks the calculations, but more importantly it checks that the program is handling the cut-off points properly.

4.6 Arrays

An array is one of the features that allow computers to process masses of data efficiently. It is a set of variables with the same name, but different index values or subscripts. The purpose of arrays is simple – by changing the subscript, the same routine can work on any or every value within an array. For example, if you wanted to collect five inputs in scalar (normal, single-item) variables, you might use lines like this:

```
user1 = InputBox("Please enter your name")
user2 = InputBox("Please enter your name")
user3 = InputBox("Please enter your name")
user4 = InputBox("Please enter your name")
user5 = InputBox("Please enter your name")
```

Using an array, you only need a single line for the inputs:

```
user[num] = InputBox("Please enter your name")
```

Another couple of lines are needed to change the value of *num* so that it works through the array, but it is still a neater solution even with only five values. Arrays are the only way to handle data in bulk.

Arrays are declared in much the same way as simple variables, but you also need to specify the *dimensions*.

```
Dim student (5) As String
```

This creates an array with one dimension and five members – *student[0]*, *student[1]*, *student[2]*, *student[3]* and *student[4]*. (Note that the index numbers start at 0.) This array might hold a list of student names.

Arrays can have more than one dimension.

```
Dim mark (30, 10)
```

This is a two-dimensional array, and could be thought of as a table. You could see this one as having 30 rows and 10 columns, and could hold the marks for 30 students and 10 assignments. *mark(5, 3)* would be the mark from the fourth assignment of the sixth student (remember that we count from 0).

To print out all the marks of all the students, you could use a block of code like the one below. (For…Next loops run through a range of values – we will look at them properly in Chapter 5.)

```
For student = 0 to 29
   For assignment = 0 to 9
      Print mark(student,assignment)
   Next assignment
Next student
```

An array can have any number of dimensions. For instance, a fully computerized warehouse facility might have 6 sheds, each of which has 4 rooms, each with 10 aisles, each with 12 stacks of 6 shelves, which are divided into 20 compartments. To set up the array for this, you would use:

```
Dim item(6,4,10,12,6,20) as String
```

And to pick out any given item, you would need an expression like this:

```
...item(shed, room, aisle, stack, shelf,compartment)...
```

Arrays in Visual Basic can be huge – you can have up to 2^{64} (that 18,000,000,000,000,000,000) elements in each dimension, and as many dimensions as you like and as your computer can handle. (If the array is too big to fit into RAM, the overflow will be stored in virtual memory, on disk, but this will dramatically reduce running speed.) In practice, it's hard to manage an array with more than half a dozen dimensions because you have to think about six things at once.

Redim

If the amount of data to be held in an array is not known in advance, and if it may change during the program's execution as different sets of data are stored and manipulated, you can use the **Redim** command to redefine the array.

```
Dim userdata(rows, columns)        'when it is first set up

Redim userdata(rows, columns)      'redefined later
```

After this line, the *userdata* array will be *rows* by *columns* in size, with whatever values these have been assigned at that point. Any existing data in the array is lost when it is redimensioned.

Ubound( )

As the dimensions of an array can be set by variables, in a large and complex program it is possible that the size of an array may not be known in a subroutine. Using a global variable to track the array size would be one solution, but Visual Basic offers a simple alternative. The **Ubound**() function gives you the upper boundary of a selected dimension in an array.

The syntax is:

```
dimension = Ubound(ArrayName, DimensionNumber)
```

For example, with a two dimension array, MyGrid(10, 25):

```
Ubound(MyGrid, 1) = 10
Ubound(MyGrid, 2) = 25
```

4.7 Variables and files

Data in variables is only there as long as the program is running. If you want to keep it for the future, you have to store it in a file on the disk. Visual Basic has some highly sophisticated facilities for handling files – most of which are beyond the level of this book – but it also gives you very simple ways to write data to and read it from a disk.

Data is written to a file through a **StreamWriter** object.

```
Dim myfile As StreamWriter = New StreamWriter("datafile.txt")
```

This creates the variable *myfile* which links the program to the file *datafile.txt*. If the file does not exist, it will be created. If it does exist, it will be opened for writing.

Data is written using the **Write()** or **WriteLine()** functions – WriteLine() sends a linefeed/carriage return at the end of each writing operation, so that the data is stored as separate lines. This can make it easier to read back – with a Write() you may have to work a little harder to get data back in later.

```
myfile.WriteLine("This is text on file")
myfile.WriteLine(surname(count))
```

The first line stores the given text, the second stores whatever is held in the *surname* array at position *count*.

Reading from a file follows the same lines. The link is through a **StreamReader** object, and is read with **Read()** or **ReadLine()**.

```
Dim myfile As StreamReader = New StreamReader("datafile.txt")
incoming = myfile.ReadLine( )
```

When you have finished with a file, it should be closed with the **Close()** function. This ensures that data is written safely onto the disk, and releases the memory that had been allocated to handling the file.

```
myfile.Close( )
```

Note that the StreamWriter/StreamReader objects and their functions are in the System.IO namespace. To use them, you must put **System.IO** in front of their names, e.g. **System.IO.Write()**, or add this line to the very top of the program:

```
Imports System.IO
```

Worked example

For this you will need to set up a form with a TextBox (mine is called *ShowTxt*) and five Buttons, labelled GetData, Display, Save, Load and Exit. The Buttons' names should reflect their labels. Set the TextBox's Multiline property to True.

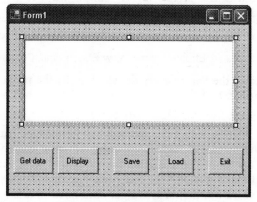

Figure 4.1   A suitable form layout for the filing worked example.

Here's the code. There are five routines:

* **GetData** collects 10 names (or other text items) into the *data()* array.

* **Display** joins them into one long string and copies them to ShowTxt.

* **Save** writes the contents of data() to the file mydata.txt. This will be stored in the program's default folder – Bin in the project's folder.

* **Load** reads the file into data().

* **Exit** ends the program.

Where the code needs to work through the array, it uses the **For…Next** structure that we met earlier. This simple demo stores and reads 10 items. With a little extra programming, it could be made to store as many items as the user desired, and to read as many as were in the file.

Type it in and test it. Use GetData, Display and Save, then Exit. Run it again, and this time start with Load, then use Display to check that the data has been read from the file.

```
Imports System.IO
Public Class Form1
    Inherits System.Windows.Forms.Form
    Dim data(10) As String
    Dim count As Short

# Windows Form Designer generated code

Private Sub GetdataBtn_Click(ByVal sender As System.Object, ByVal _
e As System.EventArgs) Handles GetdataBtn.Click
    For count = 1 To 10
        data(count) = InputBox("Enter name")     'or whatever
    Next
End Sub

Private Sub DisplayBtn_Click(ByVal sender As System.Object, ByVal _
e As System.EventArgs) Handles DisplayBtn.Click
    Dim temp As String
    For count = 1 To 10
        temp = temp & data(count) & " "
    Next
    ShowTxt.Text = temp
End Sub

Private Sub SaveBtn_Click(ByVal sender As System.Object, ByVal _
e As System.EventArgs) Handles SaveBtn.Click
    Dim datafile As StreamWriter = New StreamWriter("Mydata.txt")
    For count = 1 To 10
        datafile.WriteLine(data(count))
    Next
    datafile.Close( )
End Sub

Private Sub LoadBtn_Click(ByVal sender As System.Object, ByVal _
e As System.EventArgs) Handles LoadBtn.Click
    Dim datafile As StreamReader = New StreamReader _
("Mydata.txt")
    For count = 1 To 10
        data(count) = datafile.ReadLine
    Next
```

```
      datafile.Close( )
End Sub

Private Sub ExitBtn_Click(ByVal sender As System.Object, ByVal _
e As System.EventArgs) Handles ExitBtn.Click
    End
End Sub

End Class
```

Open or append

If you need to reopen an existing file and add more data to it, there are essentially two ways to do this:

◆ You can read the contents of the file into memory, add to them there and write the whole lot out again – and the key to this is having a variable number of items.

◆ You can append the new data to the existing file – and this needs different techniques for opening files.

These three functions from the **File** class give you more control over your files:

◆ **File.CreateText**(*path*) creates a new text file and opens it for writing – there are other functions for other types of data.

◆ **File.AppendText**(*path*) opens an existing file, and moves the writing position to the end of the file, so that new text is added after the existing data.

◆ **File.Exists**(*path*) gives a True value if the file is present.

path is the path and name of the file. It can be given directly or through a string variable.

Here are the functions at work – the If…Then structure makes the program use AppendText if the file exists, and OpenText if it does not. If…Then is explained in the next chapter.

```
Dim path As String = "C:\temp\mydata.txt"
Dim datafile As StreamWriter
If File.Exists(path) Then
    datafile = File.AppendText(path)
Else
    datafile = File.CreateText(path)
End If
```

4.8 Number operators

When calculating with numbers, you can use these arithmetic operators:

^		Exponentiation (power)
+	–	Plus and minus
\	Mod	Integer division and remainder
*	/	Multiply and divide

The integer division operators may be new to you. Integer division (\) gives the whole number of times that the number can be divided, and Mod gives the remainder. e.g.

    22 \ 5 = 4   22 Mod 5 = 2

    7 \ 3.2 = 2   7 Mod 3.2 = 0.6

The minus sign can also be used to mark a negative number.

If the expression contains more than one operator, the calculation follows the normal rules of precedence, i.e. the operators are processed in the order:

    ^ – (negative) * / \ Mod + –

For example:

    answer = 2^2 + 4 * 6 / 3 – 1

First ^ exponentiation...

    answer = 4 + 4 * 6 / 3 – 1

Next multiplication and division...

    answer = 4 + 24 / 3 – 1

    answer = 4 + 8 – 1

Then addition and subtraction...

    answer = 11

If required, you can change the order of operations by placing brackets round the ones to be performed first.

Here we go again:

    answer = 2^(2+ 4) * 6 / (3 – 1)

First the bracketed operations...

    answer = 2^6 * 6 / 2

Then ^ exponentiation...

answer = 64 * 6 / 2

Next multiplication and division...

answer = 192

Practical examples

Test the arithmetic operators by creating this little program. It allows you to input any two numbers then find the result of the arithmetic operations. First set up the form:

1 Place on a form three Text Boxes, named Number1, Number2 and Result.

2 Next place six buttons, labelling and naming them to suit the operators **+ – * / ** and **Mod**.

3 Place an exit button to give the program a tidy end.

Better layouts

The Format menu can help to tidy up the layout of controls. First select the set of controls then go into the menu.

Make Same Size is always a good one to start with!

Use the Align options to line them up vertically or horizontally.

Use the Horizontal and Vertical Spacing options to adjust the distance between them.

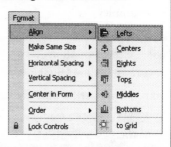

The operator buttons were all made the same size, then the top two were aligned along their tops, next the two columns were aligned – separately – on their Lefts.

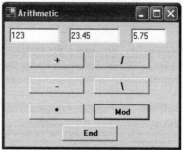

The code on all the buttons is almost the same. Here's what you need on the Plus button:

```
Result.Text = Val(Number1.Text) + Val(Number2.Text)
```

For the other buttons, simply change the operator.

The Val() function is only essential for the + operator as this can also work with text (see section 4.3). It ensures that the contents of the Text properties are treated as number values. Miss it out and you will find that 2 + 2 = 22.

4.9 Assignment operators

The arithmetic operators can be combined with the '=' sign to produce these assignment operators:

```
+=    -=    *=    /=    \=    ^=
```

These can only be used to perform a calculation on a variable and store the result back in the same variable. A simple example would be for handling a running total:

```
Total += Item
```

This is the same as:

```
Total = Total + Item
```

If you have long variable names, you will appreciate the reduction in the amount of typing:

```
UsersCurrentBankBalance -= LatestWithdrawal
```

There is also a '&=' assignment operator, which will add text onto the end of the current string:

```
Output.Text &= NextWord
```

4.10 Logical (bitwise) operators

The operators And, Or and Xor are mainly used for combining expressions in logical tests (see section 5.5), but they can also be used for manipulating numbers at a binary level.

Here's a crash course for those readers that haven't worked with binary numbers before.

Binary numbers

In any number, the value that a digit represents depends upon two things – the digit itself, and its place in the number. This is true in any number system. Look at a number in our normal (base 10) system. Take the digits of 1066, working right to left:

```
6   =   6 * 1      =      6
6   =   6 * 10     =     60
0   =   0 * 100    =      0
1   =   1 * 1000   =   1000
```

Each time you move a place to the left, the value of the digit increases by a factor of 10.

In binary (base 2) numbers, the place value increases by 2. So, in the number 10101, the digits are worth (in base 10):

```
1   =   1 * 1      =    1
0   =   0 * 2      =    0
1   =   1 * 4      =    4
0   =   0 * 8      =    0
1   =   1 * 18     =   16
```

The standard unit of computing is the byte, which has 8 bits (binary digits) and can represent any value between 0 and 255.

128	64	32	16	8	4	2	1
0	0	0	0	1	0	0	1

You can look at binary numbers in two ways. You can combine the bits to give the overall value – 9 in the last example; but you can also use the individual bits to signify on (1) or off (0) status. For instance, in Chapter 9 you will meet the **FontStyle** property of RichTextBoxes. Bold, italics, underline and strikethrough are all held in this property. They can be accessed individually, e.g.:

   …FontStyle.Bold

turns Bold on (and everything else off).

   …FontStyle.Italics

turns Italics on (and everything else off).

But in this context, **Bold, Italics** and the rest are constants, where **Bold** = 1, **Italics** = 2, **Underline** = 4 and **Strikethrough** = 8.

You must have seen where this was leading – **FontStyle** is held in a single byte, and the status of the four styles are held in its last

4 bits. You can produce composite styles by turning on several bits, e.g.

...FontStyle.5

turns on Bold and Underline (1 + 4 = 5).

You can also check and change the status of individual bits – and that is where And, Or and Xor come into play.

And

If you combine two numbers with And, the bits are compared and if the same bit is 1 in both numbers, then that bit in the result is 1.

Looking at it in binary:

1 And 1 = 1

1 And 0 = 0

It takes a little longer to demonstrate in base 10.

89 And 69 =

Convert to binary:

	128	64	32	16	8	4	2	1	
89 =	0	1	0	1	1	0	0	1	
69 =	0	1	0	0	0	1	0	1	
	0	1	0	0	0	0	0	1	= 65

We can use this to test the status of bits. Looking back to the FontStyle values, assume that you had a variable *myStyle* which held the style setting. The expression:

If (myStyle And 2) = 2 Then...

This gives a True result if the Italics bit is on.

Or

If you combine two numbers with Or, if either or both of the bits at one place are 1, then that bit in the result is 1.

1 Or 0 = 1

1 Or 0 = 1

0 Or 0 = 0

For example,

89 Or 69 =

Convert to binary:

	128	64	32	16	8	4	2	1	
89 =	0	1	0	1	1	0	0	1	
69 =	0	1	0	0	0	1	0	1	
	0	1	0	1	1	1	0	1	= 93

We can use Or to make sure that bits are set. Sticking with the FontStyle example, this expression:

myStyle = (myStyle Or 1)

will turn on Bold if it is not already on, or leave it on if it is.

Xor

This is the eXclusive Or. This only gives a 1 result if one or other – but not both – of the compared bits is 1.

1 Xor 0 = 1
1 Xor 0 = 0
0 Xor 0 = 0

For example,

89 Xor 69 =

Convert to binary:

	128	64	32	16	8	4	2	1	
89 =	0	1	0	1	1	0	0	1	
69 =	0	1	0	0	0	1	0	1	
	0	0	0	1	1	1	0	0	= 28

We can use Xor to 'flip' bits – toggling them between 1 and 0, and echoing the toggle switches that are used for on/off options. Sticking with the FontStyle example, this expression:

myStyle = (myStyle Xor 1)

will turn Bold on if it is off, or off if it is on.

Other bitwise operators

The bitwise operators, >> and << (and their assignment equivalents >>= and <<=) can also be used to manipulate numbers at a binary level. 'Bit-twiddling' can be fascinating – you are working close to the levels of the chips – but it is beyond the scope of this book.

Exercises

1 Define variables to hold these details of employees in a firm:

(a) full name,

(b) years of service,

(c) internal phone number,

(d) salary.

2 Define an array *days()* containing the names of the days of the week. Place a TextBox and a NumericUpDown (setting the Maximum to 6) on a form.

Write code in the **NumericUpDown_ValueChanged** handler to make the day names appear in the TextBox.

3 Colours can be set with **FromArgb(alpha, red, green, blue)**. This takes values in the range 0 to 255 for the colour's transparency (alpha), red, green and blue components.

Set up a form with an empty PictureBox, three HScrollBars and a VScrollBar. Use the HScrollBars to control the colours and the VScrollBar to control the transparency of the PictureBox's BackColor.

The **FromArgb** lines should look like this:

```
PictureBox1.BackColor = Color.FromArgb(alpha, red, green, blue)
```

Summary

• There are a range of data types to handle text, different ranges of numbers, dates and other objects.

• A variable is a named space in memory where data can be stored, read and changed. A variable is declared with a Dim line, specifying its name and type.

• Values are assigned to variables with the = sign.

• Where a variable is declared controls its scope – where it can be used.

• A constant is a named space in memory. Once a value has been assigned to it, it cannot be changed during the program's run.

• An array is an organized set of variables, which have the same name but are identified by index numbers.

• If you need to retain data after the end of a program, it should be written to a file.

• There is a full set of arithmetic operators for numeric calculations. These can be combined with the '=' sign to form assignment operators.

• You can use the bitwise operators, And, Or and Xor, to check or change the settings of individual bits in a byte.

05

program flow

In this chapter you will learn:

- about the flow of execution
- how to use loops to repeat processes
- about branching with If...Then and Select Case
- how to print a document

5.1 Flow of execution

The flow of execution is the order in which a block of code's statements are carried out – and this is straight across the line and from one line down to the next unless there are instructions to redirect the flow. Where the task is simple, or where there is only a single item of data to be processed, straight-through flow may well be enough, but programs would not be much use if the code was this simple. What gives programs their power is their ability to repeat operations – allowing them to process masses of data efficiently – and to perform different actions in response to different circumstances – giving them the flexibility to deal with varied situations.

Loops

A loop is a block of code that can be executed a number of times. There are three different kinds of loops, and several ways of creating each of them.

◆ An *unconditional* loop is one where the code is repeated a set number of times, e.g. to print out a multiplication table, or to produce the wage slips for every employee on the payroll. These are typically created using the **For...Next** structure.

◆ A *conditional* loop is one that is repeated if or until a certain condition is met, e.g. reading data from a file for as long as there is anything there to read, or taking inputs from the user until an acceptable value is given. These are more varied than conditional loops, and can be set up with the **Do While** or Do Until Loop structures (amongst others), testing for true or false values, and testing at the start, at the end or even in the middle of the loop.

◆ An *infinite* loop is the result of bad programming, and will hang a program and possibly crash the computer. Every loop must have an exit of some sort, somewhere.

5.2 For...Next loops

A For...Next loop will work through a range of numbers. By default, it will increment the loop counter, one at a time, but you can set it up to take larger steps, or to count down.

The basic sysntax is:

```
For Counter = start To finish [Step stepsize]
    statements
Next Counter
```

Counter must be a variable (normally a Short integer); *start*, *finish* and *stepsize* can be variables or literal values. The **Step** clause is optional. The *Counter* after **Next** can be omitted, but including it helps to make the code more readable.

Some examples. This counts from 1 to 10.

```
For Counter = 1 To 10
    …
Next Counter
```

This counts from 0 to 60, in steps of 10 – so the *Counter* values will be 0, 10, 20, 30, 40, 50 and 60.

```
For Counter = 0 To 60 Step 10
```

This counts down from 10 to 0.

```
For Counter = 10 To 0 Step -1
```

A loop demo program

The For…Next loop is a simple one to follow. Some of the other loop structures are not so obvious. So, let's build ourselves a little test bed which we can use to explore them.

Set up a form containing one label and two buttons. The label will display the Counter values as you work through the loops, so you might want to give this a larger, more visible font. You should also give it a meaningful name, e.g. *Output*.

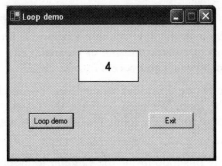

Figure 5.1 The loop testbed in action.

One of the buttons will be used to start the loop. The other is our usual 'tidy exit' button.

Double-click on the demo button to open the Code window at its Click method. Type in the code shown here:

```
Private Sub DemoButton_Click(ByVal sender As System.Object, _
ByVal e As System.EventArgs) Handles DemoButton.Click
    Dim count As Short
    For count = 1 To 10
        Output.Text = count
    Next count
End Sub
```

Build and run the program and observe. Did you see the numbers 1 to 10 displayed in the label? No? It's not surprising really, as the computer will have whistled round that loop in a fraction of a microsecond. We need to slow things down to human speed, and we need to make sure that the number is displayed each time round the loop.

There are a number of ways in which we can slow down a program, but the simplest – and most appropriate at this point – is to use another loop. We could get the computer to twiddle its thumbs by running round an empty loop like this:

```
For delay = 1 To 1000000
Next delay
```

That would help, but a modern PC can twiddle its thumbs at an impressive rate of knots. It will be more effective if we give it something to do on the way round – a bit of trigonometry should slow it down.

```
x = Math.Sin(y)
```

This uses the **Sin()** function from the **Math** class. We'll look at these a bit closer in the next chapter. Right now, it's enough to know that this calculates the sine of an angle, and it takes the PC a few microseconds to process it.

That will handle the delay, but you will still see no change until the end of the loop. We need to make the system update the screen each time round the loop. We can do that with the line:

```
Refresh()
```

We could write this loop inside the *Counter* loop, but I'd prefer to keep the demo as clean as possible. Here's a better way. When the loop changes the value in the *Output* label, the action triggers a *TextChanged* event. We can write the delay into its method.

Use the Class and Method drop-down lists to get into the label's TextChanged method, and type in the code shown here – notice the Dim lines at the start.

```
Private Sub Output_TextChanged(ByVal sender As Object, ByVal _
e As System.EventArgs) Handles Output.TextChanged
    Dim delay As Long
    Dim x, y As Double
    Refresh( )
    For delay = 1 To 1000000
        y = 0.12345        ' can be any value
        x = Math.Sin(y)    ' twiddle thumbs
    Next delay
End Sub
```

Build the program. Now can you see the numbers changing as the code goes round the loop? You may want to adjust the delay. 1,000,000 works for me, but your PC may be faster or slower.

Variable loops

A loop's start, finish and stepsize values can be set by variables. We can use that to observe how values change in loops. Edit the demo code as shown below. This sets up three variables, *start*, *finish* and *stepsize*, which get their values through InputBoxes.

```
Dim count, start, finish, stepsize As Short
    start = InputBox("Enter start value")
    finish = InputBox("Enter finish value")
    stepsize = InputBox("Enter step value")
    For count = start To finish Step stepsize
        Output.Text = count
    Next count
```

Run the program. Each time that you click the Demo button, you will be asked for a new set of values. The program has no error-checking, so it is possible to enter a stepsize that does not allow the loop to be completed, e.g. one that produces the loop:

```
For count = 1 to 10 Step 0
```

This will hang the program. The only way out is to call up the Task Manager and end the program from there!

Nested For loops

For...Next loops (or any other type) may be nested inside one another. Two loops are used in here to build a times table – the layout could be improved, but at least this shows the principles.

```
Dim outer, inner As Short
    For outer = 1 To 10
        For inner = 1 To 10
            Output.Text &= (outer * inner) & " "
        Next inner          ' end of inner loop
        Output.Text &= Chr(10) & Chr(13)
    Next outer              ' end of  outer loop
```

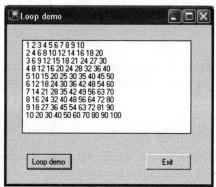

Figure 5.2 The output from this routine – note that the font size has been reduced so that we can display more numbers.

For every trip through the outer loop, this makes 10 trips round the inner loop. And what's going on inside those loops?

The *inner* loop contains only this line:

```
Output.Text &= (outer * inner) & " "
```

Let's take this from right to left: *outer * inner* multiplies the current loop values. The result is then tacked onto the end of whatever is in the **Text** property (with a following space to keep it clear of the next number) and assigned to **Text**. The overall effect is to create a line of numbers for each *outer* value.

The outer loop contains – of course – the inner loop, but also this line:

```
Output.Text &= Chr(10) & Chr(13)
```

Chr(10) is ASCII character 10, the line feed, which moves the print position down to the next line; Chr(13) is the ASCII code for Carriage Return, which moves the cursor back to the start of the line. Used together, these codes have the same effect as an [Enter] keypress.

It may be obvious, but it is worth stressing – you must end the inner loop inside the outer one. The syntax checker will tell you if the loops are out of order.

Variable nested loops

In this routine, we again have two nested loops. This time the outer loop provides the finish value for the inner loop. As the inner loop writes asterisks across the display, the effect is to draw a triangle of #s.

```
Dim outer, inner As Short
    For outer = 1 To 10
        For inner = 1 To outer
            Output.Text &= "#"
        Next inner
        Output.Text &= Chr(10) & Chr(13)
    Next outer
```

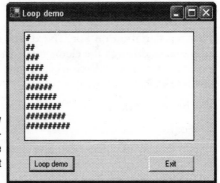

Figure 5.3 The output – how would you get a downward-pointing triangle, or one with the angled side sloping from right down to left?

Exit For

Sometimes you need to get out of a **For…Next** loop early and not work through to the finish value. **Exit For** will force an end to the loop, jumping over any lines between it and the closing **Next** line. It cannot be used by itself – stick one into the middle of your last demo and it will make the loop end early every time. It must be used with some kind of branch statement – typically **If** – so we will leave it until a little later in this chapter.

5.3 Loops and arrays

For…Next loops offer an efficient way to work through the elements in an array, with the loop counter acting as the array's index. Try this – it sets up an array for storing five names. They are collected through InputBox lines, then displayed.

```
Dim member(5) As String
Dim index As Short
For index = 0 To 4
    member(index) = InputBox("Enter name")
Next index
For index = 0 To 4
    Output.Text &= member(index) & Chr(10) & Chr(13)
Next index
```

With two nested loops, you could process the table of data in a two-dimensional array. And you need not stop at two – you can have as many nested loops as you need to work through a multi-dimensional array.

5.4 For Each…Next

This is a variation on For…Next, the difference being that this loop works through the elements in an array or a collection. We have not yet met collections, but you can just as well see how this works using an array.

The basic syntax is:

```
For Each item In array
    …
Next item
```

Where *item* is of the same data type as *array* – and not a counter to act as the index value, e.g. in the following code you will see:

```
For Each name In member
```

name is a String, to match the *member()* String array.

To access an element you use the For Each variable directly, e.g.

```
name = InputBox("Enter name")
```

instead of using an index value to identify an element, e.g.

```
member(index) = InputBox("Enter name")
```

Edit the last code to create this **For Each** demo:

```
Dim member(5) As String
Dim name As String              ' same data type as the array
For Each name In member         ' work through the array
    name = InputBox("Enter name") ' instead of member(index)
Next name
For Each name In member
    Output.Text &= name & Chr(10) & Chr(13)
Next name
```

5.5 Making comparisons

Relational operators

Before we move on to the other types of loops and then to branches, we need to look at how we can compare values as comparisons are used to determine the direction of program flow.

Visual Basic has six relational or comparison operators, which can be used to test the values in variables.

=	Equals	<>	Not equal
<	Less than	<=	Less than or equal to
>	More than	>=	More than or equal to

They can be used on both numeric and string variables.

Numeric testing it obvious, though it is worth noting that you can compare different types of numeric data, e.g. Single and Short variables.

Whether a string is 'greater than' or 'less than' another depends upon the ASCII code of its characters, not its position in the alphabet. For example 'A' (ASCII code 65) is less than 'B' (ASCII 66) and less than 'a' (ASCII 97).

```
num1 <= 99
```

This expression results in a Boolean value of True if *num1* is less than or equal to 99, and False if *num1* is more than 99. The result of a test can be assigned to a Boolean variable – and this can help to improve the readability of your code. For example:

```
overdrawn = (balance < 0)
if overdrawn then ...
```

Logical operators

A comparison operator can only test one variable or value against another. If you need to compare two or more values, you need to link the test with logical operators. There are two key ones – **And** and **Or**.

And

If you have two or more sets of values and each test must be true, they should be linked with And. For example:

   ...(age > 15) And (age <= 65)...

This test will prove true when the *age* value is between 16 and 65 inclusive.

Notice that each comparison operation has been enclosed in brackets. These are not essential, but they do help to make the program more readable by emphasizing the individual tests.

You can have any number of comparisons linked by Ands. This expression, for example, tests that the *x* and *y* values are within the limits of a 100×100 grid:

   ...(x>=0) And (x <=100) And (y>=0) And (y <=100)...

Or

Or is used to link tests when you want any one or all of them to be true. For example:

   ...(age <= 15) Or (sex = "f") Or (sex = "F") ...

This will pick out the women and children.

And and Or operators can be combined if needed. For example, this will select men over 65 and women over 60:

   ... ((age > 65) And (sex = "M")) Or ((age > 60) And (sex = "F")) ...

Note the second level of brackets to keep each test together. They are not actually necessary here as And tests are checked before Or tests, but they do help to clarify the expression.

If you want an Or test to be done before an And, you must enclose it in brackets.

   ... (sex = "M") And ((age < 16) Or (age > 65)) ...

This is true if the subject is a young boy or an older man.

Miss out the brackets and what happens?

    ... (sex = "M") And (age < 16) Or (age > 65) ...

This now selects boys and older people of either sex.

Not

This reverses the truth of a test.

    ... Not (password = "letmein") ...

is the same as:

    password <> "letmein"

Look what happens when you use Not with And and Or. These two expressions have the same effect:

    ... Not ((age > 15) And (age <= 65)) ...

    ... (age <= 15) Or (age >65) ...

Not can be used with Boolean variables to produce more readable code. If you have a variable *overdrawn* which is True when the balance is below 0, then you can have this expression:

    Not overdrawn

which tells you clearly that there is money in the bank.

5.6 Do...Loops

There are four varieties of the **Do...Loop** structure. All repeat a block of code subject to a test of some sort. The test can be at the beginning or at the end of the block, and the block can be repeated until the test proves true, or while it is true.

Do...Loop Until

With **Do...Loop Until/While** structures, the test is at the end, so that the program always passes through the loop at least once.

    Do
    ...
    Loop Until *test is true*

The **Until** version checks to see if a key value has changed so that the test is now true. For example, has the right password been given?

Write this into the **Form_Load** subroutine of your test program:

```
Dim password As String
Do
    password = InputBox("Enter password")
Loop Until password = "letmein"        ' set your own password!
```

Build and run the program. You should find that you cannot get past the InputBox without giving the right password.

Do...Loop While

A **While** test checks to see if a value is still true – the opposite of an **Until** test. Try this:

```
Dim age As Short
Do
    age = InputBox("How old are you?")
Loop While ((age < 0) Or (age > 114))
```

This loop ensures that a valid age is entered. (At the time of writing, the oldest living person was 114.)

The **While** test picks up an invalid age. We could run the check with an **Until** test, if we looked for a valid age. This line has exactly the same effect – and its meaning is more obvious:

```
Loop Until ((age >= 0) And (age <= 114))
```

It doesn't matter then whether you use a **While** or an Until test – choose whichever gives you more readable code.

Do Until/While...Loop

In these next two versions, the test is at the start of the loop.

```
Do Until test is true
    ...
Loop
```

If the test is true when the program flow first reaches it, then the code in the loop will not be executed at all.

```
Do Until balance <= 0
    payout = InputBox("How much do you want to spend?")
    balance -= payout
Loop
```

This could equally well have been written with a **While** test:

```
Do While balance > 0
    payout = InputBox("How much do you want to spend?")
    balance -= payout
Loop
```

Exit Do

If necessary you can leap out of a loop part way through, using the **Exit Do** statement. This is virtually same as **Exit For** and can likewise only be used alongside a branching statement – it is typically written in an **If...Then...** line. So, let's have a look at branching now, and we'll get back to the early exits later.

5.7 If...Then...

If...Then... is the main branching structure in Visual Basic. At the simplest, the syntax is:

```
If (test is true) Then statements
```

The statements following **Then** are only performed if the test is true, e.g.

```
If x > 100 Then x = 100
```

This chops x back to 100 if it goes over the limit.

There can be any number of statements after **Then**. They must be separated by colons.

```
If x > 100 Then x = 100 : y = 0 : MsgBox("Overrun!")
```

In practice, it is best to use the single-line **If...** only when there is a single statement. Where there are several things to do, you get more readable code by using this block version of the structure.

```
If (test is true) Then
    statements
    ...
End If
```

Here, everything between the **Then** and the **End If** is executed if the test is true. That last example could be written like this:

```
If x > 100 Then
```

```
    x = 100
    y = 0
    MsgBox("Overrun!")
End If
```

Notice that there is no punctuation at the ends of the lines – the colon is only needed where the statements are on one line.

If...Then...Else

What if the test is not true? With the basic If, the program flow moves on to the next line or the line after the End If. This code will also be performed if the test is true. Sometimes that is what you want. Other times, you want one set of code to be executed if the test is true and another set if it is false.

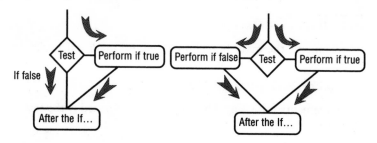

Figure 5.4 With a simple If, an extra block of code is performed if the test is true, then the flow returns to the same place.

If...Then...Else gives you that structure. The basic syntax is:

```
If (test is true) Then
    statements if true
Else
    statements if false
End If
```

Or

```
If (test is true) Then
    statements if true
Else : statements if false
End If
```

If you write the statement(s) on the same line after an Else, Visual Studio will put a colon after Else when it checks the line.

For example, a very polite program might greet its users:

```
If (sex = "F") Then
    MsgBox("Good day, madam")
Else
    MsgBox("Good day, sir")
End If
```

ElseIf

If two branches are not enough, you can add more with the **ElseIf** clause. This tacks another **If…Then…** onto an **Else**.

```
If (test1 is true) Then
    statements if true
ElseIf (test2 is true) Then
    statements if true
Else
    statements if both tests are false
End If
```

Note that the program flow skips to the end of the whole structure after performing a set of **Then…** statements. As a result, even if several tests are true, only the code from the first true test will be executed.

Try this trivial demonstration. Write it into your test button.

```
Dim salary As Double
salary = InputBox("Annual salary please")
If (salary > 2000000) Then
    MsgBox("Can I have your job")
ElseIf (salary > 200000) Then
    MsgBox("I wouldn't complain about that either")
ElseIf (salary > 20000) Then
    MsgBox("You obviously don't write for a living")
Else
    MsgBox("Time to retrain")
End If
```

Type it in and see what happens when you enter salaries across the range of values. Reverse the order of the tests, so that 20,000 is first and 2,000,000 is last. What happens now when you enter different salaries?

5.8 Loop and branch game

It's time to put some of these loop and branch structures to work. The next example uses an If...Then...ElseIf... and a Do Loop Until structure to create a simple guessing game. The program generates a random number which the user has to guess. The code displays messages if the guess is too high or too low, and loops round until the number is guessed correctly.

There are two minor points to note.

```
Dim NL As String = Chr(10) & Chr(13)
```

This gives us a convenient way of handling new lines. Having stored both characters in a variable, we can then simply tack NL onto a string when we want to mark the end of a line.

```
x = Int(Rnd() * 100) + 1
```

This generates a random whole number in the range 1 to 100. (Actually it is produced by a calculation so is not truly random, but the numbers are unpredictable and spread evenly across the range, so it is random enough for most purposes.)

The **Rnd**() function produces a random fractional value between 0 and 1, e.g. 0.456789. This is then multiplied by 100.

Int() turns the value into an integer by cutting off the decimal fraction. The number will now be in the range of 0 to 99. We need to add 1 to make it 1 to 100.

```
Dim x, guess, tries As Short
    Dim NL As String = Chr(10) & Chr(13)    'new line
    Output.Text = ""          ' start new game
    tries = 0
    x = Int(Rnd() * 100) + 1     ' random number between 1 and 100
    Do
        tries += 1
        guess = InputBox("Guess my number")
        Output.Text &= guess & " "
        If guess > x Then
            Output.Text &= "Too high" & NL
        ElseIf guess < x Then
            Output.Text &= "Too low" & NL
        Else
            Output.Text &= "Success!" & NL
        End If
```

```
Loop Until guess = x
Output.Text &= "That took " & tries & " goes"
```

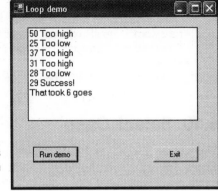

Figure 5.5 You should always be able to guess the number in no more than 7 goes. Why?

5.9 Early Exits

We can now put the **Exit For** and **Exit Do** statements to work. The repetition of a **For...Next** loop is controlled solely by the value of the counter; on a **Do Loop** it is controlled (normally) by the value of a single While/Until test variable. Sometimes, a change in the value of another variable means that you need to break out of a loop.

For example, the loop that we used to check the password could go round for ever if the password is not known. It would be better if we restricted users to a set number of tries, then either throw them off completely or take them through a registration routine, or whatever.

Here's how we can do it with an **Exit Do**.

```
Dim password As String
Dim tries As Short = 0    ' declare variable and set it to 0
Do
    tries += 1
    if (tries > 3) Then Exit Do
    password = InputBox("Enter password")
Loop Until password = "letmein"        ' set your own password!
If tries > 3 Then ... ' doesn't know the password routine
```

And here's another approach – this uses an **Exit For**.

```
Dim password As String
Dim tries As Short
For tries = 1 To 3
    password = InputBox("Enter password")
    if (password = "letmein") Then Exit For
Next tries
If (password <> "letmein") Then ... ' doesn't know the password
```

5.10 Select Case

You can have as many **ElseIf** clauses as you like within an **If...Then...Else** structure, but if you want to branch in a lot of different ways depending upon the value in a variable, **Select Case** is a neater alternative.

The basic syntax is:

```
Select Case variable
    Case value or value range1
        statement(s)1
    Case value or value range2
        statement(s)2
    ...
    [Case Else
        statement(s) ]
End Select
```

When the program goes into a **Select Case** structure, it looks at the value in the named variable. If this matches the value or range of values after a **Case** keyword, the following statements are executed. The flow then moves out of the structure. If a **Case Else** is used, its statements are executed if the variable's value does not match any of the Case values.

Try this simple example. Write it into your test button.

```
Dim letter As String
letter = InputBox("Enter a letter A to D")
letter = UCase(letter)  'convert to upper case
Select Case letter
    Case "A"
        MsgBox("A is for Apple")
    Case "B"
```

```
        MsgBox("B is for Banana")
    Case "C"
        MsgBox("C is for Cherry")
    Case "D"
        MsgBox("D is for Date")
    Case Else
        MsgBox("Out of range")
End Select
```

The variable can be of any simple data type, e.g. Boolean, Short, Double, String, etc., but not arrays or other compound types.

Case values can be defined in three ways:

- Given directly, with commas between if more than one value is specified, e.g. to match upper of lower case "A".

    ```
    Case "A", "a"
    ```

- As a range, using **To**, e.g. to match any capital letter,

    ```
    Case "A" To "Z"
    ```

- As a comparison, prefixed by the keyword Is, e.g. to match numbers over 99.

    ```
    Case Is > 99
    ```

Case values are defined in all three ways in this next example.

```
Dim letter As String
letter = InputBox("Type a character")
Select Case letter
    Case "A" To "Z"          ' range of values
        MsgBox("Uppercase letter")
    Case "a" To "z"
        MsgBox("Lowercase letter")
    Case "0" To "9"
        MsgBox("Digit")
    Case " "                 ' single value
        MsgBox("Space")
    Case Is < " "            ' comparison test
        MsgBox("Non-printing character")
        ' Enter keypress, arrow keys, etc
    Case Else
        MsgBox("Symbol")
End Select
```

Let's have one last example. This demonstrates that Select Case doesn't just work with Strings. The Case variable in this routine is an Integer.

```
Dim num As Integer
    num = InputBox("Enter a number")
    Select Case num
        Case 3, 7
            MsgBox("Lucky number")
        Case 13
            MsgBox("Unlucky number")
        Case 0 To 9
            MsgBox("Single digit")
        Case Is > 10000
            MsgBox("Big number")
        Case Is < 0
            MsgBox("Negative number")
        Case Else
            MsgBox("Between 10 and 9999, but not 13")
            ' all other values have been covered in the Cases
    End Select
```

Exercises

1 Mathematicians love series. The triangle number series is what you get if you add up the counting numbers (1, 2, 3, 4...) but including one more each time. This gives you 1, 3, 6, 10, etc.

Write a routine to calculate any given number in the series, using a For...Next loop.

2 A club sets these membership fees.

Junior (16 or under) = £20 p.a.

Adult waged = £50, unwaged £30

Over 65 waged = 40, unwaged = £25

There is a 10% discount for direct debit. Write the code to determine the fees for a new member.

3 Create an address book, to store names and e-mail addresses, saving the data as a file. It should be able to display one name and e-mail at a time, and have routines to move through the list. New data should be added through a separate routine. Use For...Next and Do Loops to control repetition.

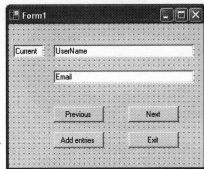

Figure 5.6 A possible layout for the controls needed in Exercise 3.

Summary

- **For...Next or For Each...Next loops allow you to repeat an action for a set number of times or work through a series of values.**

- **Text and numeric values can be compared to see if they are the same as, greater or less than each other. The results of the tests are Boolean values.**

- **Do...Loops can be controlled by Until or While tests, at the beginning or end of the loop. The type of test and its position affect the way that the loop repeats.**

- **If necessary, you can leap out of any loop using an Exit.**

- **The flow of execution can be directed down different branches using an If...Then...Else structure.**

- **Where there are many possible branches, all arising from the state of one variable, Select Case can give a neater structure than If...Then...Else.**

06

subroutines and functions

In this chapter you will learn:

- how to create your own subroutines and functions
- how to pass data into and out of subroutines and functions
- about the Math methods

6.1 Subroutines and functions

We've been using subroutines – and a few functions – for five chapters now, but without thinking too much about them, so perhaps it is time that we looked at them seriously.

Subroutines

So far, the only subroutines that we have seen have been event-handlers – linked to objects and activated when an event occurs to that object. Subroutines can also be free-standing blocks of code, with specific links to any object.

The basic shape of a subroutine is:

```
Private Sub subName(arguments)
    statements
End Sub
```

The *arguments* are variables used to pass data between the subroutine and the other parts of the program.

This simple subroutine shows the times table for a given number.

```
Private Sub TimesTable(ByVal base As Short)
    Dim count As Short
    Output.Text = ""
    For count = 1 To 10
        Output.Text &= base & " * " & count & " = " * (base * count)
        Output.Text &= Chr(10) & Chr(13)  'new line
    Next
End Sub
```

Testing subroutine definition

You might want to start a new project for this chapter. If not, clear any existing code from your test project. You need a form with a Button, for starting your code, and a Label for output.

To define a subroutine:

1 Double-click on the Button to go into the Code window.

2 We are not writing the button code yet. Place the cursor after the **End Sub** and press [**Enter**] to open a blank line.

3 Type **Private Sub** and the rest of the header line for the subroutine.

4 Press [**Enter**] at the end of the line. A blank line will appear, with an **End Sub** line below it.

5 Type the code for the subroutine between the header and the **End Sub** lines.

Calling a subroutine

If a subroutine is activated, or 'called', from elsewhere in the program, the calling line will have this shape:

```
subName(variables)
```

To call the *TimesTable* subroutine to display the 7 times table we would therefore use the line:

```
TimesTable(7)
```

Or you could display a table of the user's choice, with this code. Type it into Sub Button_Click to test it:

```
Dim num As Short
num = InputBox("Enter number")
TimesTable(num)
```

We'll look closer at how arguments are defined and used shortly.

Subroutines without arguments

A subroutine does not have to have arguments. It may work with global variables, or not use data from elsewhere in the program. In this case, place empty brackets after the name when defining the subroutine, e.g.

Private Sub NoArgs( )

and when calling it:

NoArgs( )

Early Exits

You can leave a subroutine before the end, in the same way that you can break out of a loop. The command is

```
Exit Sub
```

and it would be used after an **If** or in a **Select Case** structure.

Functions

The key difference between a function and a subroutine is that a function 'returns' a value – it generates a value which is passed back into the program. Think of a maths function such as Sine. It would be written into an equation like this:

```
x = sin(y)
```

A function can be used wherever a value or variable can, and like a variable it must have a data type. The basic shape is then:

```
Private Function functionName(arguments) As datatype
    statements
    functionName = return_value
End Function
```

Notice the line, beginning *functionName*... Every function must have such a line, to store the calculated value in the function for passing out to the calling code.

Here is an example of a simple function:

```
Private Function Cube(ByVal num As Double) As Double
    Dim temp As Double
    temp = num * num * num
    Cube = temp                    ' store the value in the name
End Function
```

This takes a Double value passed from the program, cubes it and passes it back as the function result. The function is defined as Double. It could be used in lines like these:

```
x = Cube(y)
```

```
Output.Text = Cube(number)
```

Functions can be very compact – *Cube*, for example, could be written in a single line:

```
Private Function Cube(ByVal num As Double) As Double
    Cube = num * num * num
End Function
```

End lines

If you make a mistake when writing the header line of a sub or function, Visual Studio will not write the End line for you .

6.2 Passing arguments

You will have noticed each argument here has started with **ByVal**. We could have used **ByRef**. These keywords determine how data is passed into and out of a subroutine or function.

ByVal

ByVal is short for 'by value'. When data is passed by value, the *value* in the variable in the calling code is copied into the argument. Whatever is done to the argument in the subroutine or function, the value in the original variable is not changed.

ByRef

This is short for 'by reference'. When data is passed by reference, the *address* of the variable in the calling code is copied into the argument. In effect, the variable becomes the argument and if the value in the argument is changed, then the value in the variable will be changed when the program flow returns to the calling code.

ByVal and ByRef demonstration

This next example shows what happens when data is passed by value and by references. It has two subroutines, which both add 1 to the value passed in from the calling code. The main code can be written into Sub Button _Click.

Type in the code as shown.

```
Private Sub Button1_Click(ByVal sender As System.Object, ByVal _
e As System.EventArgs) Handles Button1.Click
    num = 99
    MsgBox("At the start num = " & num)
    ByValSub(num)
    MsgBox("After the call to ByValSub num = " & num)
    ByRefSub(num)
    MsgBox("After the call to ByRefSub num = " & num)
End Sub

Private Sub ByValSub(ByVal x As Short)
    MsgBox("On entry x = " & x)
    x += 1
    MsgBox("On exit x = " & x)
End Sub
```

```
Private Sub ByRefSub(ByRef x As Short)
    MsgBox("On entry x = " & x)
    x += 1
    MsgBox("On exit x = " & x)
End Sub
```

Build and run the program. Observe the messages carefully and compare them with the code. You should see that the value is increased *within* both of the subroutines. In the calling code, it is unchanged after the variable has been passed to *ByValSub* but changed after it has been through *ByRefSub*.

6.3 Using subroutines

Why use subroutines and functions in our programs? There are two key reasons:

* **Readability** – it can be difficult to follow the logic and flow of code through long solid blocks. Breaking code into smaller, clearly labelled blocks makes it easier for you and others to see what a program is doing.

* **Avoiding repetition** – if you want to perform the same set of tasks at several points in a program, it is more efficient to write the set into a subroutine. This can then be called from any and many lines thoughout the program. For example, in most Windows applications users can often access routines from toolbar buttons and from menu selections. Instead of duplicating the same code in the button and the menu item's methods, you could write it into a separate subroutine, and call that from the button and menu item's Click methods.

Though subroutines and functions are all but identical in how they work, you should only use a function where the purpose of the code is to acquire or calculate a single value of some sort – and nothing else. For anything else, use a subroutine.

Example project: EasyCalc

This next project is a simple calculator – it only handles basic arithmetic and has no memory or correction facilities. It is mainly here to demonstrate subroutines in action, but it may also serve as a guide to developing programs.

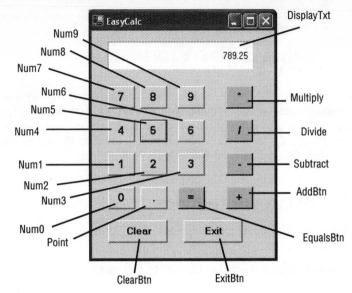

Num9

Num8

Num7

Num6 — DisplayTxt

Num5

Num4

Num1

Num2

Num3

Num0

Point

Multiply

Divide

Subtract

AddBtn

EqualsBtn

ClearBtn

ExitBtn

Figure 6.1 The layout for the EasyCalc program, showing the names used in the program code.

We want something that looks and behaves like a pocket calculator, so we should start by looking closely at how they work.

Number buttons

Numbers are, obviously, entered through the number pad, and this is straightforward to handle. At the start, or if an operator or the Equals button have just been pressed, then we will need to start a new number, otherwise we just add the appropriate digit to the display when a button is clicked. That leads us to this code, in the *processDigit()* subroutine:

```
Private Sub processDigit(ByVal digit As Short)
    If newnum Then
        display.Text = digit
        newnum = False
    Else
        display.Text &= digit
    End If
End Sub
```

If *newnum* is True, the program expects a new number to be entered and so the incoming *digit* replaces whatever may be in the display; *newnum* is then set to False. When the next *digit* is entered, it is added to the end of the existing display number.

processDigit() is an example of how subroutines produce more efficient code. This handles the inputs from all 10 of the number buttons. The only code on the Click event-handler of a Num is the single line that calls the subroutine, passing to it the appropriate value. This is *Num1*'s code. The rest are virtually the same.

```
Private Sub Num1_Click(ByVal sender As System.Object, ByVal e
As System.EventArgs) Handles Num1.Click
    processDigit(1)
End Sub
```

Notice that the decimal point has its own code for writing "." into the display. If *processDigit()* had been written to take the digit as a String, instead of as a Short, then the point could also have been passed to it.

Operator buttons

When an operator button is pressed, the number in the display is stored, the operation to be performed is also stored, and the calculator gets ready to take in the next number. When the user presses the equals or another operator button, then the current number is combined with the stored value and the result copied into the display.

There are three possible situations, and they are handled in the *processOp()* subroutine.

* An operator key is pressed, but there is no number in the display. In this case, we simply need to store the operator.

```
If newnum Then
' if last operator was = and no number yet entered
    op = operator        ' then simply store next operator
    Exit Sub
End If
```

We could have made this the first part of an extended **If...Then...ElseIf...** structure, but as there is nothing else that we need to do in the subroutine, an **Exit Sub** offers a neater solution.

* There is no pending operation – i.e. at the very start or if the last operation was an equals, which would have performed

the calculation. Let's suppose that there is 23 in the display and the user had just pressed [+]. We need to store the number in the display and store the operator.

That gives us this code:

```
If (op = 0) Or (op = 5) Then
    'no operation yet recorded - first number in display
        n1 = Val(display.Text)
        op = operator
```

op is the stored operator; 0 indicates just started or cleared; 5 shows equals was the previous operation. In this example, at the end of this code *op* would have 1, to indicate addition, and *n1* would hold 23.

◆ There is a number and an operation in store, and the second number in the display. We need to get the latest number, and run the stored operation on the two values. The result is then written back into the display and the new operation stored. That gives us this code:

```
n2 = Val(display.Text)
Select Case op
' process the operator entered between the numbers
    Case 1 : n1 += n2 ' 1 = add
    Case 2 : n1 -= n2 ' 2 = subtract
    Case 3 : n1 *= n2 ' 3 = multiply
    Case 4 : n1 /= n2 ' 4 = divide
End Select
display.Text = n1
op = operator ' store operator
```

If our user had 10 in the display at the start and had pressed [=], as the stored *op* is 1, *n2* would have been added to *n1*. At the end, the display would show 33, and *op* would be 5.

The operator buttons pass the operation code as they call the subroutine, e.g.

```
Private Sub Multiply_Click(ByVal sender As Object, ByVal e As
System.EventArgs) Handles Multiply.Click
    processOp(3)
End Sub
```

There is one other subroutine: *clear()* is called on Form_Load, i.e. at the start of the program, and when the Clear button is clicked. This clears the display, zeros *n1* and *n2*, and sets *newnum* to True, ready to start a new calculation.

```
Private Sub clear()
    display.Text = ""
    n1 = 0
    n2 = 0
    newnum = True
End Sub
```

The EasyCalc code

```
Public Class Form1
    Inherits System.Windows.Forms.Form
    Dim n1, n2 As Double
    Dim op As Short
    ' code for last selected operation 0 none 1 + 2 - 3 * 4 / 5 =
    Dim newnum As Boolean

    # Windows Form Designer generated code
    ' produced when controls are placed on the form

    Private Sub processdigit(ByVal digit As Short)
        If newnum Then
            DisplayTxt.Text = digit
            newnum = False
        Else
            DisplayTxt.Text &= digit
        End If
    End Sub

    Private Sub Num0_Click(ByVal sender As Object, ByVal e As _
    System.EventArgs) Handles Num0.Click
        processdigit(0)
    End Sub

    Private Sub Num1_Click(ByVal sender As Object, ByVal e As _
    System.EventArgs) Handles Num1.Click
        processdigit(1)
    End Sub

    Private Sub Num2_Click(ByVal sender As Object, ByVal e As _
    System.EventArgs) Handles Num2.Click
        processdigit(2)
    End Sub
```

```vbnet
Private Sub Num3_Click(ByVal sender As Object, ByVal e As _
System.EventArgs) Handles Num3.Click
    processdigit(3)
End Sub

Private Sub Num4_Click(ByVal sender As Object, ByVal e As _
System.EventArgs) Handles Num4.Click
    processdigit(4)
End Sub

Private Sub Num5_Click(ByVal sender As Object, ByVal e As _
System.EventArgs) Handles Num5.Click
    processdigit(5)
End Sub

Private Sub Num6_Click(ByVal sender As Object, ByVal e As _
System.EventArgs) Handles Num6.Click
    processdigit(6)
End Sub

Private Sub Num7_Click(ByVal sender As Object, ByVal e As _
System.EventArgs) Handles Num7.Click
    processdigit(7)
End Sub

Private Sub Num8_Click(ByVal sender As Object, ByVal e As _
System.EventArgs) Handles Num8.Click
    processdigit(8)
End Sub

Private Sub Num9_Click(ByVal sender As Object, ByVal e As _
System.EventArgs) Handles Num9.Click
    processdigit(9)
End Sub

Private Sub Point_Click(ByVal sender As Object, ByVal e As _
System.EventArgs) Handles Point.Click
    If newnum Then
        DisplayTxt.Text = "."
        newnum = False
    Else
        DisplayTxt.Text &= "."
    End If
End Sub

Private Sub processOp(ByVal operator As Short)
    If newnum Then        ' if no number yet entered
```

```
        op = operator          ' then simply store next operator
        Exit Sub
    End If

    If (op = 0) Or (op = 5) Then
    'no operation yet recorded - first number in display
        n1 = Val(DisplayTxt.Text)
        op = operator
    Else
        n2 = Val(DisplayTxt.Text)
        Select Case op
        ' process the operator entered between the numbers
            Case 1 : n1 += n2
            Case 2 : n1 -= n2
            Case 3 : n1 *= n2
            Case 4 : n1 /= n2
        End Select
        DisplayTxt.Text = n1
        op = operator ' store operator
    End If
    newnum = True
End Sub

Private Sub AddBtn_Click(ByVal sender As Object, ByVal e As _
System.EventArgs) Handles AddBtn.Click
    processOp(1)
End Sub

Private Sub Subtract_Click(ByVal sender As Object, ByVal e As _
System.EventArgs) Handles Subtract.Click
    processOp(2)
End Sub

Private Sub Multiply_Click(ByVal sender As Object, ByVal e As _
System.EventArgs) Handles Multiply.Click
    processOp(3)
End Sub

Private Sub Divide_Click(ByVal sender As Object, ByVal e As _
System.EventArgs) Handles Divide.Click
    processOp(4)
End Sub

Private Sub EqualsBtn_Click(ByVal sender As Object, ByVal e _
As System.EventArgs) Handles EqualsBtn.Click
    processOp(5)
```

```
End Sub

Private Sub clear()
    DisplayTxt.Text = ""
    n1 = 0
    n2 = 0
    newnum = True
End Sub

Private Sub ClearBtn_Click(ByVal sender As Object, ByVal e As _
System.EventArgs) Handles ClearBtn.Click
    clear( )
End Sub

Private Sub Form1_Load(ByVal sender As Object, ByVal e As _
System.EventArgs) Handles MyBase.Load
    clear( )
End Sub

Private Sub ExitBtn_Click(ByVal sender As System.Object, ByVal _
e As System.EventArgs) Handles ExitBtn.Click
    End
End Sub

End Class
```

6.4 Using functions

Let's add some functions to our calculator. If it is to be used for 'proper' maths, then it should at least be able to calculate sine, cosine, tangent, powers and square roots. We can work out some of the simpler ones for ourselves. For the others we can draw on Visual Basic's ready-made mathematics functions.

The Math methods

The Math class is one of several built-in classes whose methods (normally functions) and fields (predefined constants) are available to the programmer. You can bring them into your programs in two ways.

* If you only want one or two methods from a class, specify the class as part of the method, e.g. to use **Sin**() from the **Math** class, you would write something like:

```
answer = Math.Sin(angleA)
```

- If you want several methods, it is simpler to import the whole class into the program. Its methods can then be accessed by their name alone. Type this before the **Public Class** line:

```
Imports System.Math
```

Then when a method is needed:

```
answer = sin(angleA)
```

We will use this method – add the line now.

Angles: degrees and radians

As is normal in programming languages, the Math trigonometry functions measure angles in radians, not degrees.

If you need to work in degrees, the conversion is not difficult. A full circle is 360° or 2 Pi radians – and Pi is a constant defined in the Math class (to a level of accuracy far higher than any of us ever needs). That gives the formulae:

$$\text{degrees} = \frac{\text{radians} * 2 * \text{Pi}}{360} \quad = \quad \frac{\text{radians} * \text{Pi}}{180}$$

$$\text{radians} = \frac{\text{degrees} * 360}{2 * \text{Pi}} \quad = \quad \frac{\text{degrees} * 180}{\text{Pi}}$$

Our first two functions are based on these formulae:

```
Private Function DegToRad(ByVal degrees As Double) As Double
    DegToRad = degrees * Pi / 180
End Function

Private Function RadToDeg(ByVal radians As Double) As Double
    DegToRad = radians 180 / Pi
End Function
```

To incorporate these into our program we need to do two things: create the functions themselves – simple enough, just type them into the existing code; and provide a way to activate them.

Extending the calculator

We are going to need more buttons – you'll also need more space on the form. Make the form deeper so that there is room for two or three more rows (we will be adding the trigonometry and power functions later). I've placed the new buttons at the top – but the layout is entirely up to you. If you use the same names as I have (see Figure 6.2) it will make it easier to follow the code.

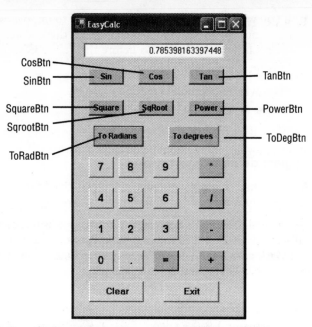

Figure 6.2 The revised layout for EasyCalc, with the new buttons added.

To use our new functions, we simply pass across the value in the display. A couple of minor tweaks are needed around this: we should check that there is a value to work on; and we should set *newnum* to True so that the next time a digit button is clicked, it starts a new number.

The **Click** subroutines of the **ToRad** and **ToDeg** buttons are virtually identical:

```
Private Sub ToRad_Click(…        'line cropped to fit in the book
   If Val(DisplayTxt.Text) <> 0 Then
      DisplayTxt.Text = DegToRad(Val(DisplayTxt.Text))
   End If
   newnum = True
End Sub

Private Sub ToDeg_Click(…
   If Val(DisplayTxt.Text) <> 0 Then
      DisplayTxt.Text = RadToDeg(Val(DisplayTxt.Text))
   End If
   newnum = True
End Sub
```

Square and Power functions

We can write these ourselves. The code for the square function is trivial – it just multiplies the incoming value by itself and passes the result back:

```
Private Function square(ByVal n As Double) As Double
    square = n * n
End Function
```

Its calling code on the Square button is the same as that on ToRad, except for the name of the function:

```
DisplayTxt.Text = Square(Val(DisplayTxt.Text))
```

Raising a number to a power has all sorts of complexities if the power has a decimal fraction. An integer power is much easier, so we'll limit ourselves to that. (This is not a maths textbook!) All we need to do now is multiply the number by itself for as many times as the power value.

The function takes in two numbers – the *base* and the *power*. These come in as floating point variables, though *power* is later converted to an integer by the **Round()** function – one of the methods in the Math class. *temp* starts with a value of 1, and is repeatedly multiplied by *base* through a **For** loop. The result is then copied into the function name at the end.

```
Private Function intPower(ByVal base As Double, ByVal power As _
Double) As Double
    Dim count As Short
    Dim temp As Double = 1
    For count = 1 To Round(power)
        temp *= base
    Next
    intPower = temp
End Function
```

As our *intPower* function needs two numbers, we cannot handle this the same way as the earlier ones. Instead we have to treat this as an operation. The **Power** button calls up the *processOp* subroutine, setting the op to 6.

```
processOp(6)
```

And within the Select Case, we add this line:

```
Case 6 : n1 = intPower(n1, n2)
```

Method	Returned value
Abs(x)	The absolute value of x, i.e. ignoring the sign, e.g. Abs(-4) = 4.
Acos(x)	The angle whose cosine is x.
Asin(x)	The angle whose sine is x.
Atan(x)	The angle whose tangent is x.
Atan2(x, y)	The angle whose tangent is the quotient of x / y.
BigMul(x, y)	64-bit Long result of multiplying x and y, two 32-bit Integers.
Ceiling(x)	The smallest whole number greater than or equal to x.
Cos(x)	The cosine of x.
Cosh(x)	The hyperbolic cosine of x.
DivRem(x, y, rem)	The quotient of two numbers; the remainder passed as a parameter, e.g. howmany = DivRem(x, y, remainder).
Exp(x)	*e* raised to the power of x; the constant *e* is also defined.
Floor(x)	The largest whole number less than or equal to x.
IEEERemainder(x, y)	The remainder resulting from x / y, where both are Doubles.
Log(x)	The natural logarithm of x.
Log10(x)	The base 10 logarithm of x.
Max(x, y)	The larger of x and y.
Min(x, y)	The smaller of x and y.
Pow(x, y)	x raised to the power of y.
Round(x)	The whole number nearest to x.
Sign(x)	-1 if x is < 0; 0 if x = 0; 1 if x is > 0.
Sin(x)	The sine of the given angle.
Sinh(x)	The hyperbolic sine of the given angle.
Sqrt(x)	The square root of a given number.
Tan(x)	The tangent of the given angle.
Tanh(x)	The hyperbolic tangent of the given angle.

Figure 6.3 The Math methods.

The ready-made Math functions are used in exactly the same way as our home-made ones – the only difference is that you will not see the function code in your program. For example, the **Sine** button code should look like this:

```
Private Sub SinBtn_Click(...
    If Val(DisplayTxt.Text) > 0 Then
        DisplayTxt.Text = Sin(Val(DisplayTxt.Text))
    End If
End Sub
```

I'll leave you to add the rest.

6.5 Recursion

Recursion is an intriguing and important programming technique. It involves calling a function from within itself, so it is basically circular – though there must always be an escape route!

Factorials offer a good opportunity to demonstrate recursion. For the benefit if non-mathematicians, a factorial number is a whole number that is multiplied by every other one lower than it. They are used a lot in probability calculations. A factorial is indicated by ! (shriek) after the number, e.g. 4!

Look at the start of the factorial sequence.

```
1! = 1
2! = 2 * 1           or      2 * 1!
3! = 3 * 2 * 1       or      3 * 2!
4! = 4 * 3 * 2 * 1   or      4 * 3!
```

You can calculate any factorial by multiplying the number by the factorial of the next lower number. This works all the way down to 1!, which is 1. We can turn this into pseudo-code:

if the number is 1, then the factorial is 1

else the factorial is the number multiplied by the factorial of the next lower number.

And go from there to proper code:

```
Private Function factorial(ByVal x As Integer) As Integer
    If (x = 1) Then
        factorial = 1
    Else
        factorial = x * factorial(x - 1)
    End If
End Function
```

If you first call the function with the expression **factorial(3)**, it will produce the expression **3 * factorial(2)** – calling itself. The next time round, it generates **2 * factorial(1)**, and calls itself again. This time it finds the answer 1, and returns the value to the previous call, which uses this to calculate the value 2, and returns that to the top level. At this point the function does 3 * 2, and comes up with 6 which it passes back to the program.

Exercises

1 Give the calculator memory functions so that it can store and recall a number, add a value to memory and subtract a value from memory.

2 Add functions to the calculator to allow it to work out any power or root. Hint: use the Log() and Exp() methods.

Summary

- Subroutines and functions are self-contained blocks of code. The same block can be called (executed) from any number of places in the project.

- The call to a subroutine is a simple statement.

- A function returns a value. This can be assigned to a variable or used within an expression.

- Data can be passed into and out of subroutines and functions through arguments.

- The Math methods are a ready-made set of mathematical functions and constants.

- A recursive function is one which calls itself.

07
dealing with errors

In this chapter you will learn:

- about types of errors
- how to use the debugging tools
- about trapping errors to prevent program crashes

7.1 Errors and error spotting

Even the best programmers make mistakes! Fortunately, the Visual Studio provides excellent tools for finding and correcting errors. There are three main categories of error.

• **Syntax errors** are mistakes in the way that the language is used – typically misspelling keywords, giving the wrong type of data to a function, or missing out part of a command. These are usually spotted by the system, either when you move the cursor off the line or when it builds the program.

• **Logical errors** occur when you use the words and structures correctly, but don't quite manage to say what you mean. Visual Basic has no means of identifying these, and unless the error crashes the program or produces visibly strange results, you will not be aware of them yourself. Commercial software is all too often released with bugs that only show up when the programs are pushed to their limits by users. To ensure that you have found and cured all logical errors, you must design a thorough testing procedure that will explore every possible route through the program, and every possible combination of values. Any problems thrown up by the testing can then be investigated using the debugging tools.

• **Runtime errors** can occur because of unexpected external events, e.g. the user inputs the wrong type of data, or the program attempts to load a non-existent file or communicate with a detached peripheral. You cannot prevent these, but you can prevent them from crashing your program.

Scanning for errors

When you are writing your code, as soon as you press [Enter] at the end of the line, or move the cursor off it, the line is scanned for errors. If one is found, it is given a wavy blue underline. Point at it and a pop-up box will tell you what's wrong. This will usually point out missing keywords or other punctuation, but will sometimes give a less-than-helpful 'Syntax error' message.

If no errors are found, the line is rewritten in a standard format. Spaces are inserted around symbols, and those words that the system recognizes as being part of the Visual Basic vocabulary are forced into mixed upper and lower case and recoloured. Do check the revised line. A misspelt keyword will occasionally fail to produce an error message, because the system assumes you mean something entirely different. If a word has not been reformatted, first check its spelling, then check your quotes. One or other will almost certainly be the cause of the problem.

Compile-time error reports

The line scan will pick up errors on individual lines and check the syntax of **If, Case, Loop** or similar structures, though it may not always pick up errors in more complex structures. The ones that the scanner missed or that you failed to notice will be picked up when the Studio attempts to build the project.

If you see this:

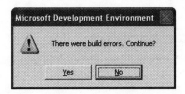

Click **No** to return to the Code window. At the bottom of the window you will see a panel listing the errors. These are usually identified by line number – and line numbers are not normally displayed in the Code window.

To display line numbers:

1 Open the **Tools** menu, and select **Options**.

2 Click on Basic in the left pane.

3 Tick **Line numbers** in the **Display** area.

Runtime error reports

There are some errors that will slip through these nets, but bring the program crashing to a halt at some point during its execution. Typically these errors revolve around data types – the data that you are attempting to pass from one variable, function or control to another is of the wrong type for its target. A second common cause is trying to use a control, a file or other object which doesn't exist. You may have misspelt the name, or changed it, or deleted the object during an earlier edit.

If you are running the program from within the Studio, the line where the error occurred will be highlighted in green in the Code window. The error will be reported in a message box, offering you the options to **Break** or **Continue. Continue** closes down the program, and opens the Code window at the point where you were last working. **Break** takes you into debugging mode, where you can examine the code and your variables.

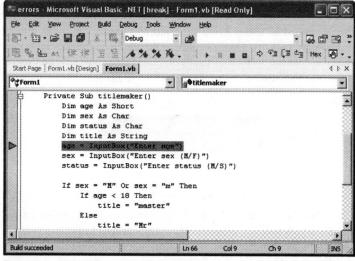

Figure 7.1 This program built successfully, but crashed when running. Taking the Break option brought us to this display. The highlighted line is the one being executed when the error occurred.

If you are running the program from its .exe file, outside the Studio, then you will get a slightly different error message box. Click the **Details** button to get more details, make a note of them and head back to the Studio to sort out the problem.

List your variables

You will find it easier to deal with these kind of errors if you have a list of the controls and variables. A moment's reference to the list can save an hour's searching through the code. Being organized really does help!

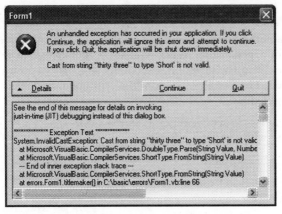

Figure 7.2 An error message from a free-standing VB program.

7.2 Debugging tools

The best debugging tools are a piece of paper and a pencil. Use these to design your program, to list your variables and to dry run the design. Use them thoroughly and you won't have (m)any bugs, or much need for Visual Basic's debugging tools. These can be accessed through the Debug menu or the Debug toolbar. (Right-click on the Standard toolbar and tick **Debug** to display the toolbar.)

If you are getting odd results and cannot understand where they are coming from, break into the program. Use **Run > Break All**, the ▣ button or **[Ctrl]-[Break]** to suspend the program and go into debugging mode. A green highlight in the code will show you what was being executed when you broke in – though this will only be useful if a routine was active at that moment.

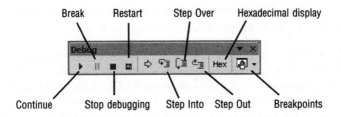

7.3 Breakpoints

Breakpoints allow you to bring a program to a halt at a predefined point in a procedure. When you set a breakpoint in a line of code and run the program, execution will halt when it reaches that line. The Breakpoints window will open, with the current line highlighted.

It is simplest to set breakpoints in the Code window while you are editing.

To set a breakpoint:

1 Right-click on the line where you want to break.

2 Select **Insert Breakpoint**.

The line will be given a red highlight and a blob placed by its side.

To remove breakpoints:

1 Click on the red blob by the line in the Code window.

Or

2 Click ✖ in the Breakpoints window.

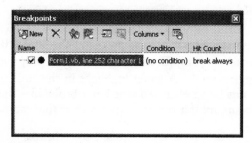

Figure 7.3 The Breakpoints window. New Breakpoints can also be set up from here.

Any number of breakpoints may be set, and **Debug > Clear All Breakpoints** will remove them all when the bugs have been ironed out. In practice you would rarely want more than two or three at once, as too many interruptions make it difficult to follow the flow of the program. Use breakpoints to track down one bug at a time, placing one at the last point where you know the code is good, and another further on. After running the program and checking the state of crucial variables when each breakpoint is reached, you can then bring them closer together, repeating the process until you have identified the troublesome block or line of code.

7.4 Keeping watch

A *watch* will track the values of variables, the properties of controls or the results of calculated expressions. Here is a trivial example. When I run this sums program, it keeps telling me that the answer is wrong, when it is clearly right.

The relevant line reads:

```
If textbox1.text + textbox2.text = textbox3.text Then
    feedback.text = "Right!"
```

The simplest way to set a watch is during debugging.

To set a watch:

1 Run the program to a breakpoint or break in at a suitable time.

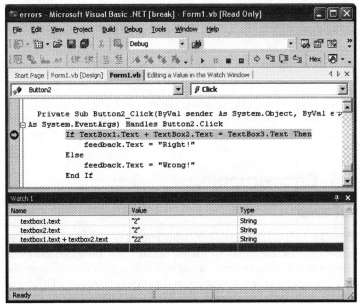

Figure 7.4 And now I see the error of my ways.

2 Open the **Debug** menu, point to **Windows**, then to **Watch**, then select **Watch1** (or other ones to add further watches).

3 In the Watch window, type the name of a variable or control or type an expression in the **Name** column.

The current value in the variable or the result of the expression based on current values will be shown in the **Value** column, with the data types in the **Type** column.

7.5 Stepping through

Sometimes the best way to see what is happening in a program is to slow it down to a speed at which you can follow it. For this we have the Step commands. They can be used as a way of starting execution, or restarting after a break.

♦ **Debug > Step Into** (or 📷) will execute one line at a time, allowing you to use a Watch to check the progress of variables as you go.

♦ **Debug > Step Over** (or 📷) will execute normally any sub or function called from within the one you are stepping through. This contrasts with **Step Into**, which would go off and work through the called routine, line by line.

♦ **Debug > Step Out** or the 📷 icon will complete the current routine normally.

In stepping, the Code window opens, and the relevant line is highlighted as it is executed. As this will probably obscure the active form, be ready to switch between them as you step.

7.6 Error-trapping

On Error

The **On Error** statement can trap run-time errors. Use this to track down errors and to guard against the program crashing when users fail to behave as expected. It is particularly valuable in filing operations, as it can trap the 'File not found', 'Drive not ready' and other common – and fatal – mistakes that can occur when accessing drives.

Errors can only be trapped within a sub or function, so if you have several places at which fatal errors are possible, each must have its own routine.

The syntax takes the form:

```
Sub ....
    On Error GoTo labelled_line
    ...
Exit Sub

labelled_line:
    display error message or counteract problem
Resume label or Next
```

On Error must be early in the code, before the potential source of error. The *labelled_line* and handling-code will typically be at the end. To avoid running into this by mistake, force an early end with **Exit Sub**.

How you handle the error is entirely up to you. If the purpose of the routine is to pick up flaws in the design during debugging, then the most sensible thing to do is to display a message box telling you what the error is. This can be found from the **Err** object. Its properties include Number, Source and Description which together can identify the error very clearly.

```
On Error GoTo errmess
...
errmess:
MsgBox ("The error is " & Err.Description & " Error number " _
& Err.Number & " originating from " & Err.Source)
...
```

If the routine is there to idiot-proof the final program, then it should identify the error and either give a user-friendly message or substitute a default value, before returning to the main code. In either case, the routine must include a **Resume** statement. This tells the computer where to restart the flow of execution.

```
Resume Next
```

This will pick up from the line following the one that produced the error. If you are using this, you should first deal with the error – perhaps by substituting a default value for the one your user failed to supply. In many cases, the error will have occurred when getting a filename or other value from the user, and the procedure will not be able to continue without a valid input. Here the best solution is to tell your user what the problem is, then Resume at a label placed past the relevant lines or at the end of the procedure.

For example:

```
Private Sub AgeGroup( )
    Dim age As Short
    Dim status As String
    On Error GoTo errorlines
    age = InputBox("Please enter your age")
    If (age > 16) and (age < 65) Then
        status = "Regular"
    Else
        status = "Concession"
    End If
Exit Sub

errorsub:
    MsgBox ("Invalid number given")
    Resume endline
endline:
End Sub
```

Try...Catch...Finally

This is used for trapping *exceptions* – errors thrown up by the system – and is very similar to On Error. The basic shape is:

```
Try
    code that may produce errors
Catch
    code to deal with errors
Finally
    back to main program flow
```

A simple Catch responds to all errors, but the **Catch** line can specify the type of exception, and there can be any number of them, each dealing with a different type, e.g.

```
Catch CastErr As InvalidCastException
    code to deal with invalid type casting
Catch ArgsErr As ArgumentException
    code to deal with invalid arguments
Catch
    code to deal with all other errors
```

Summary

- Syntax errors – mistyped words or misused commands – are spotted by the line scanner and the compiler.

- The tools on the debugging menu and toolbar can help you to track down logical and runtime errors.

- By setting breakpoints you can stop the program at selected places. You can then examine the values held by variables in a Watch window.

- Stepping through code can help to pinpoint the place where it goes wrong.

- By enclosing code in On Error GoTo... or Try...Catch, you can trap and skip over errors that might otherwise cause a program to crash.

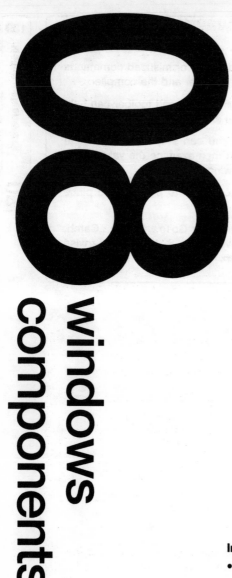

08

windows components

In this chapter you will learn:

- about standard features for Windows applications
- how to create menus
- how to set up a toolbar, with text and icons
- about Open, Save, Print and Print Preview dialog boxes

8.1 The Windows way

From the earliest versions of Windows, Windows applications have shared features that have made them instantly identifiable. Key among these are menus, toolbars and the dialog boxes that are used for handling files, printing and other routine tasks.

For the most part, they are very easy to implement, because so much is done for you. For example, to add a file-saving routine, all you need to do is bolt on the ready-made Save dialog box. It takes, literally, two minutes, though you might spend another 10 bedding it down with some user-friendly checks and prompts.

Introducing Wordless

The program that we will use to explore these features is a simple text editor – I've called it Wordless, because it offers rather less than Word. By the end of this chapter you will be able to create, save and open files with it. We'll add some formatting and editing facilities to it in Chapter 9 to turn it into a (rather basic) word-processor.

Start with a new, blank form and add a **RichTextBox** to it – this will give us more scope for formatting than a standard TextBox. You will find the control in the Toolbox, part way down the

Windows Forms set. Make it as big as the form – and set its **Anchor** property to Top, Left and the **Dock** to Fill (pick the central block). This ensures that it fills the window even if the user changes the window size. I have named this *Workspace*.

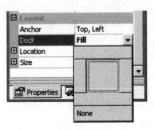

8.2 Menus

The **MainMenu** control adds a menu bar to an application. To add it, simply drop the control onto the form – don't bother about trying to locate it carefully as it knows where to go. There are two visible results: at the top of the form you will see a menu bar, blank apart from a grey "Type Here" message on the left; and a tray appears at the bottom of your workspace, with the MainMenu component placed on it.

There are three aspects to setting up a menu system:

- Creating the structure of main menus and submenus.

- Setting the names, options and other properties of the items.

- Writing the code to be activated by the menu choices.

We need **New, Open, Save, Print** and **Exit** options on a **File** menu for our simple text editor. When we later convert it into a word-processor, we will need **Edit** and **Format** menus.

Building a menu structure

A new heading or item for a menu or submenu can be added wherever you see "Type Here".

When typing the menu entries, one of the letters – usually the first – should be set so that it is underlined and can be selected by the [Alt] key combination. To do this, type an ampersand (&) before it. When you move on to the next item, the & will disappear and the letter will be underlined.

Watch out for duplication! You cannot use the same selecting letter twice in the same menu.

To start a new main menu:

- Type the heading in the menu bar. A new "Type Here" will appear beside it (for the next main heading) and below it (for a menu item).

To add an item to a menu:

- Type below the existing items.

To start a new submenu:

- Select the entry that leads to the submenu then type the first item in the "Type Here" to its right.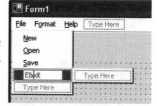

To insert a separator line:

- Right-click on the item below where the separator is to go, then select **Insert Separator** from the pop-up menu.

To edit a menu entry:

- Click on it once to select it, then again to place the typing cursor into it and edit as normal.

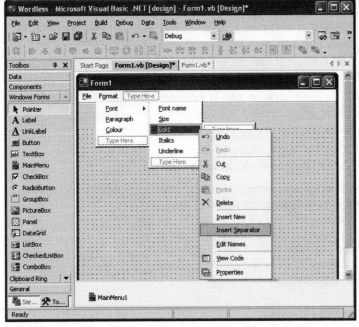

Figure 8.1 A main menu under construction.

To move a menu entry:

- Click on it and drag it to its new position.

To stop work on the menus:

- Click anywhere else on the form.

To restart work on the menus:

- Click on any heading in the menu bar.

Setting properties

At this stage you have the shape of the menus and the text for the entries, but little else. Each item has allocated a name such as *MenuItem1*, *MenuItem2*, etc., which will not help when you start to add their code – they must be clearly identified.

To rename a menu item:

1 Select the item on the menu.

2 Locate the **Name** field in the **Properties** window.

3 Replace the allocated name with a meaningful one.

While you are at the Properties window, you can also set the options. There are two key ones to note:

* **Checked** puts a tick by the entry, to show that an on/off option is on.

* **RadioCheck** puts a round bullet by the entry, to show that this is the chosen option from the set.

These options should be set to True at design time, if the default settings are on. Otherwise they can be set during run-time. We will look at Checked and RadioCheck options in Chapter 9, when we put them to use in formatting text.

Adding code

When the user selects a menu item, whether by clicking or using an [Alt] key combination, it triggers a **Click** event. The menu command's code could be written directly there, but if you want to be able to activate the same command from a toolbar button – and we do with many of ours – it is better to write the code in a separate subroutine. In this case, the item's Click event simply calls the subroutine, e.g. my **File > New** command leads to this:

```
Private Sub FileNew_Click(…     'line cropped for display
   newFile( )
End Sub
```

8.3 Context menus

A context menu is built in almost the same way as a main menu. The main differences are that the menu must be linked to an object and there can only be one main list of options.

To create a context menu:

1 Select the **ContextMenu** control from the Toolbox – you will find it towards the bottom of the Windows Forms set.

2 Drop the control anywhere on the form. The component will appear on the tray at the bottom of the window, and the prompt 'Context Menu' will temporarily replace any existing headings in the menu bar.

3 Add your menu items – starting submenus if required – in the 'Type Here' prompts.

4 Set the names and other properties, and add code as for ordinary menu items.

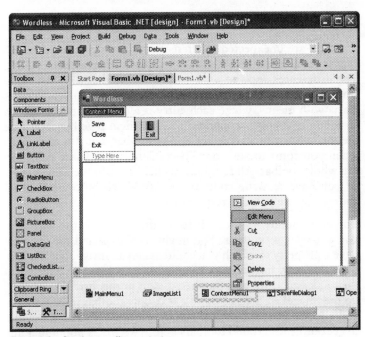

5 Click anywhere off the menu when you have done. The main menu headings will reappear.

6 If you need to edit the context menu later, click on its icon or label in the component band. The menu will again replace the main menu. Right-click on the label and select **Edit Menu**, or click directly into the displayed menu.

Figure 8.2 Starting to edit a context menu.

7 Select the control that the context menu is to pop-up from.

8 In the Properties window, click into the ContextMenu field, drop down its options and select the context menu.

◆ If you want context menus on a number of components, you can create a new menu for each (the simple solution) or set up one 'dynamic' menu where the contents alter to suit the selected control. Look up dynamic context menus in the Help system if you want to pursue this approach.

8.4 Toolbars

Toolbars are unexpectedly different from menus – not visually, that is expected, but in the way that they are created and used. The differences seem to arise from the fact that a toolbar is a single item, and its buttons are segments within it – which contrasts with menus, where each entry is a separate item, and the structure is simply a container to hold them together. You can see this when you start to set up the toolbar, but it is also clear when you come to add code. There is only one Click event for the whole toolbar. All tool button clicks lead to the same place, so you have to write code to identify which button has been clicked, before you can respond to it.

The other oddity – at least it feels odd to me – is the way that you put images on tools. You might have expected the tools to have a property to which you could assign an image, but it is not done this way. Instead, you have to set up a separate ImageList, then link each tool to a numbered item in this list. You can set up the ImageList first, or build a text-only toolbar to begin with and add the images later. We'll start with just text, as we ought to get our heads around toolbars before we worry about making them pretty.

To add a toolbar:

1 Select the **Toolbar** control from the Toolbox – you will find it just below the ContextMenu control.

2 Drop the toolbar onto the form. It will automatically locate itself just below the menu bar.

To add tools to the toolbar:

1 Select **Buttons** in the Toolbar's Properties window and click 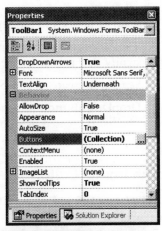. The ToolBarButton Collection Editor will open.

2 Click **Add**. The first button will appear in the Members: list.

3 Type the **Text** to be displayed on the button, and the **ToolTip Text**, if required.

4 Repeat steps **2** and **3** until all the buttons are in place.

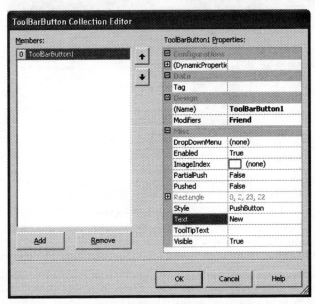

Figure 8.3 The Collection Editor as the first button is being defined.

5 Click **OK** to close the Collection Editor window.

The toolbar, waiting for its images

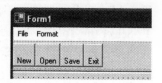

Button styles

The default toolbar button style is **PushButton,** but there are three other options in the **Style** field:

- **ToggleButton,** makes it into an on/off switch. If you want to signify that it is on at the start, set **Pushed** to **True**.

- **Separator** creates a gap between the buttons.

- **DropDownButton** attaches a drop-down list to the button. The list is created in a context menu, which is linked to the button by selecting it in the **DropDownMenu** field.

The Image Editor

Before you can put an image list together, you need to find or create the images.

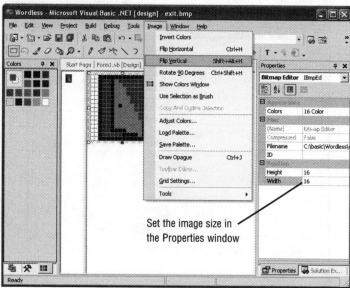

Set the image size in the Properties window

Figure 8.4 Drawing a toolbar button image in Image Editor. The tools on the toolbar and the Image menu are almost identical to those of Paint. Experiment – you'll soon get the hang of them.

You can create your own images using the Visual Studio Image Editor (or even Windows Paint or any graphics package) – though it may make you appreciate the design skills that have gone into other people's icons. The ideal image should be a clear reminder of the purpose of the button, it should look good and you must be able to draw with a 16 × 16 grid of dots! If it is the right size and different from the other button images, that will do.

To create an icon image in the Image Editor:

1 Open the **File** menu, point to **New** and select **File**.

2 At the **New File** dialog box, select Bitmap File as the type.

3 The Image Editor will open in the main workspace, with a new toolbar above it and a palette on the far left. You will also note that there is now an **Image** menu.

4 The default image size is 48×48 pixels. Change this to 16×16 in the Properties window.

5 Create your image, using the 'life-size' copy on the left as a guide to how it really looks.

   The tools are almost identical to those of Paint, but note that the third button from the right line holds the options for line thickness or drawing style of all tools.

   You are limited to 16 colours, but you can define them yourself. Double-click on a colour in the palette to edit it.

6 When you are finished, use **File > Save Bitmap As...** to save the image for use in your image list. Leave the file type at the default .BMP – the GIF and JPEG save options are there in case you want to produce images for web pages.

If you want to get your image list started quickly, there are some standard images for the filing, and the cut and paste commands, tucked away deep in the Visual Studio folder. The exact location will depend upon your system, but it should be something like:

```
C:\Program Files\Microsoft Visual Studio .NET 2003\SDK\v1.1\ _
QuickStart\winforms\samples\controlreference\tooltipctl\vb
```

If you can't find the folder down this path, you can locate it by running a search for one of its images – try looking for *clsdfold.bmp* (the Closed Folder image).

ImageLists

Creating an image list is similar to creating a toolbar – this is another collection.

1 Select the **ImageList** control from the Toolbox – you will find it just below the RichTextBox.

2 Drop it onto the form – it will go into the component tray.

3 Locate the **Images** field in the Properties window and click ▦. The **Image Collection Editor** window will open.

4 Click Add. At the **Open** dialog box, find and open the first file.

5 Repeat step **4** to add as many images as needed for the toolbar.

6 The images are easier to handle if they are in the same order as the buttons – use the ▲ and ▼ to put them into order.

7 Click **OK** to close the Editor.

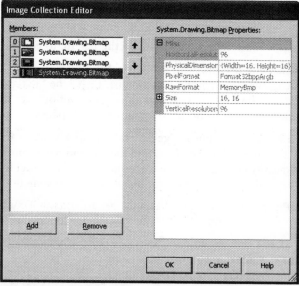

Figure 8.5 The Image Collection Editor with four images in place.

The final stage of creating the toolbar is to link the images to the buttons. This is done through the Toolbar control.

1 Select the toolbar and go to the Properties window.

2 Click into the **ImageList** field and select your newly-created ImageList from its drop-down list.

3 Click on the **Buttons** field to open the ToolBarButtons Collection Editor.

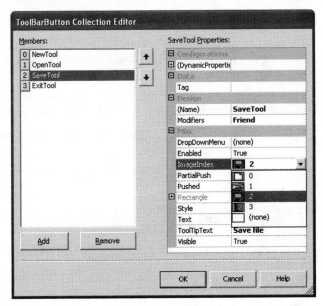

4 Click on a tool in the **Members:** list.

5 Drop down the options for its **ImageIndex** property – this links to your ImageList.

6 Select an image.

7 Repeat steps **4** to **6** as required.

8 Click **OK** to close the Editor.

Figure 8.6 A toolbar with images added – all except the Exit images are from the supplied set.

Code for toolbars

As you will remember, a toolbar has only one Click event. How then do you know which button has been clicked? The answer lies in this parameter of the Click event:

```
ByVal e As System.Windows.Forms.ToolBarButtonClickEventArgs
```

The argument *e* stores the information generated by the **Click** event. The most important part of this is in the **Button** property, which identifies the button that was clicked. The expression:

```
ToolBar1.Buttons.IndexOf(e.Button)
```

gives the number of the button, counting from 0. That can then be used in an **If...Then...** or **Select Case...** structure to direct the flow to the appropriate code.

Here's the toolbar's Click event sub, in skeleton form. The *'new routine* and similar comments will be replaced by code later.

```
Private Sub ToolBar1_ButtonClick(ByVal sender As System.Object, _
ByVal e As System.Windows.Forms.ToolBarButtonClickEventArgs) _
Handles ToolBar1.ButtonClick
    Select Case ToolBar1.Buttons.IndexOf(e.Button)
        Case 0 :    ' new routine
        Case 1 :    ' open routine
        Case 2 :    ' save routine
        Case 3 :    ' exit routine
    End Select
End Sub
```

8.5 Dialog boxes

The Toolbox contains half a dozen components, which produce standard Windows dialog boxes for standard operations: filing, printing, and setting fonts and colours. We will use the **Open** and **Save** dialog boxes in this chapter. The two are very similar – which you would expect as they are two sides of the same coin.

The Open dialog box

The Open dialog box will collect the filename from the user. It does not actually open the file – that is a different matter. But first, we need to add one to the form.

1 Select the **OpenFileDialog** control from the Toolbox – you will find it towards the bottom.

2 Drop it onto the form – it will go into the component tray, with a default name of OpenFileDialog1.

Now we need to bring it into the code. You can make the dialog box appear with this statement:

```
OpenFileDialog1.ShowDialog( )
```

But that won't get you very far. It is more useful to embed it in the expression:

```
If OpenFileDialog1.ShowDialog( ) = DialogResult.OK Then...
```

This displays the dialog box, and waits until the user has selected the file and pressed OK.

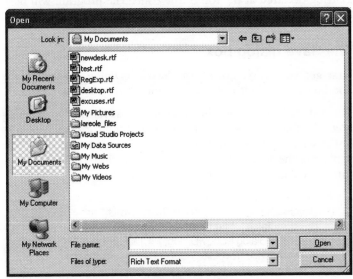

Figure 8.7 The Open dialog box, with a Rich Text filter.

Any of the dialog box's properties can be set before it is called, or read afterwards. In practice, all you really need is the resulting **FileName**. This is passed to the Open method of the control into which the file is to be loaded. In this case, it is going into the RichTextBox called *Workspace*, and RichTextBoxes have a **LoadFile** method. That give us the line:

```
Workspace.LoadFile(OpenFileDialog1.FileName)
```

It is often useful to set the Filter property, which determines the file types to display. The filter has two parts: the description and the *.extension, these are written in quotes, separated by a bar:

```
OpenFileDialog1.Filter = "Rich Text Format|*.rtf"
```

Let's put these lines together to get our file opening routine.

```
Private Sub open()
    OpenFileDialog1.Filter = "Rich Text Format|*.rtf"
    If OpenFileDialog1.ShowDialog() = DialogResult.OK Then
        Workspace.LoadFile(OpenFileDialog1.FileName)
        MyFileName = OpenFileDialog1.FileName
    End If
End Sub
```

Notice that the filename is stored in the variable *MyFileName* – a String declared at the top of the code. The program will need to know what the file was called when it is time to save it again.

The Save dialog box

First get your box. Locate the **SaveFileDialog** control in the Toolbox and drop it into the component tray.

The code for this follows the same pattern as for the Open dialog box. The Filter can be set beforehand to limit the display to files of the selected type, and you may prefer to give your own **Title** in place of the default 'Save As'. Once **OK** is clicked, the **FileName** can be passed to the *Workspace*'s **Save** routine.

```
Private Sub save()
    SaveFileDialog1.Filter = "Rich Text Format|*.rtf"
    SaveFileDialog1.Title = "Save document"
    If SaveFileDialog1.ShowDialog() = DialogResult.OK Then
        Workspace.SaveFile(SaveFileDialog1.FileName)
        MyFileName = SaveFileDialog1.FileName
    End If
    saved = True
End Sub
```

I've added a couple of tweaks. The filename is stored for use when the file is resaved, and the Boolean variable *saved* is set to True. This is set to False when the text is changed, allowing us to check if the file needs saving before it is closed:

```
If Not saved Then... ' save routine
```

8.6 Printing

Printing is one of the trickier areas of computing. Taking data formatted for output to one complex machine, reformatting it and copying it out to another complex machine is inevitably going to raise difficulties. Unfortunately, Visual Basic does not make it any easier.

Printing revolves around the Print Document in general and its PrintPage method in particular. The Print Document is where the data is assembled for output to the printer; the PrintPage method is the routine which assembles the data – and you have to write its code yourself. The example given here will handle a single page of plain text. Printing multi-page formatted documents raises problems way beyond the scope of this little book.

Start by placing a **PrintDocument** control on your form – it will drop into the component tray. If you double-click on it, you will be taken into its **PrintPage** method in the Code window.

The arguments to PrintPage include *e*, the **PrintPageEventsArgs**, which define the object to be printed. This is a **Graphics** object, and to get text into it, we need to use the **DrawString** method. This has the form:

```
e.Graphics.DrawString(text, font, brush, xPos, yPos)
```

where *text* is the text to print, *font* defines the name, size, style, etc. of the font, *brush* sets the colour and *xPos*, *yPos* define the top left corner of the print area on the paper. These can be written directly into the method, or handled through variables. In this case, the *text* and *font* are copied from the properties of *Workspace*, and *xPos* and *yPos* take their values from the margins of the PrintDocument. The *brush* needs different treatment. It is created as a new object of the SolidBrush class, with its colour set to black (or whatever), like this:

```
Dim myBrush As New SolidBrush(Color.Black)
```

Put that all together and we have a very basic PrintPage routine.

```
Private Sub PrintDocument1_PrintPage(ByVal sender As System. _
Object, ByVal e As System.Drawing.Printing. PrintPageEventArgs) _
Handles PrintDocument1.PrintPage

    Dim yPos As Single = e.MarginBounds.Top
    Dim xPos As Single = e.MarginBounds.Left
```

```
Dim printFont As Font = Workspace.Font
Dim myBrush As New SolidBrush(Color.Black)

e.Graphics.DrawString(Workspace.Text, printFont, myBrush, _
xPos, yPos)
End Sub
```

If you simply want to print to the default machine, with the default settings, then all you need is to run the PrintDocument's Print method:

```
PrintDocument1.Print( )
```

Write that into the Print button on your Toolbar or the File > Click menu item, and see what happens.

The Print dialog box

Drag a **PrintDialog** control from the Toolbox into the component tray before you do anything else.

Like the Open and Save dialog boxes, this collects data from the user and feeds it back into the code. Much of the feedback is invisible. The choice of printer, number of copies and the like are passed between the PrintDialog and PrintDocument objects through the PrinterSettings automatically. All we have to do is set up the link between these components at the start.

Our revised Print routine, using the dialog box, looks like this:

```
PrintDialog1.Document = PrintDocument1
If PrintDialog1.ShowDialog( ) = DialogResult.OK Then
    PrintDocument1.Print( )
End If
```

Print Preview

If your print routine is working, then setting up a print preview is a piece of cake. The PrintPreviewDialog does everything for you – all you need to do is bring the control onto your form (it will go into the tray with the other dialog boxes), and write a little bit of code to link the PrintDocument to it. Here's the print preview routine in its entirety!

```
PrintPreviewDialog1.Document = PrintDocument1
PrintPreviewDialog1.ShowDialog( )
```

8.7 Wordless: simple word processing

Much of the code of this program has been dealt with in detail already; some of the rest is trivial and should need no further explanation. The *checksave()* routine is worth a mention. This is called up before starting a new file, opening one or exiting from the program. It checks the *saved* variable, and offers the user the chance to save the file if it has been edited.

You might also notice that the **Save** toolbar button can respond in two different ways. If the file has already been saved – and so has a filename – clicking the button resaves it without further ado, but if there is no filename, the button calls up the save routine. This is how most Windows **Save** buttons work. If we really want to follow the Windows standard, we should make the **Save** menu entry work the same way, and add a **Save As** menu entry to allow an existing file to be saved with a new name. I'll leave you to do that for yourself.

The Toolbar code assumes that you have six buttons: New, Open, Save, Print, Print Preview and Exit. If you have more or less than this, or they are in a different order, you must change the Case numbers to suit.

```
Public Class Form1
    Inherits System.Windows.Forms.Form
    Dim saved As Boolean = False        ' global variable
    Dim MyFileName As String = ""       ' global variable

#Region " Windows Form Designer generated code "

Private Sub ToolBar1_ButtonClick(ByVal sender As System.Object, _
ByVal e As System.Windows.Forms.ToolBarButtonClickEventArgs) _
Handles ToolBar1.ButtonClick
    Select Case ToolBar1.Buttons.IndexOf(e.Button)
        Case 0
            newFile( )
        Case 1 : open( )
        Case 2
            If MyFileName <> "" Then
                Workspace.SaveFile(MyFileName)  ' resave current file
                saved = True
            Else
                save( )                   ' go to the Save dialog box
            End If
```

```
        Case 3 : printout( )
        Case 4 : printPreview( )
        Case 5 : SaveAndExit( )
    End Select
End Sub

Private Sub newFile( )
    checksave( )                    ' save current file?
    Workspace.Text = ""             ' clear the text area
End Sub

Private Sub open( )
    checksave( )                          ' save current file?
    OpenFileDialog1.Filter = "Rich Text Format|*.rtf"
    If OpenFileDialog1.ShowDialog( ) = DialogResult.OK Then
        Workspace.LoadFile(OpenFileDialog1.FileName)
        MyFileName = OpenFileDialog1.FileName
    End If
End Sub

Private Sub save( )
    SaveFileDialog1.Filter = "Rich Text Format|*.rtf"
    SaveFileDialog1.Title = "Save document"    ' optional title
    If SaveFileDialog1.ShowDialog( ) = DialogResult.OK Then
        Workspace.SaveFile(SaveFileDialog1.FileName)
        MyFileName = SaveFileDialog1.FileName
    End If
    saved = True
End Sub

' checksave( ) called by new( ), open( ) and SaveAndExit( )
Private Sub checksave( )
    Dim saveNow As Short            ' result from MsgBox
    If Not saved Then
        saveNow = MsgBox("Save the file?", 4, "Save file?")
        If saveNow = 6 Then save( )
    End If
End Sub

Private Sub SaveAndExit( )
    checksave( )
    End
End Sub

' menu commands
Private Sub FileNew_Click(ByVal sender As Object, ByVal e As _
System.EventArgs) Handles FileNew.Click
```

```
    newFile( )
End Sub

Private Sub FileOpen_Click(ByVal sender As System.Object, ByVal _
e As System.EventArgs) Handles FileOpen.Click
    open( )
End Sub

Private Sub FileSave_Click(ByVal sender As System.Object, ByVal _
e As System.EventArgs) Handles FileSave.Click
    save( )
End Sub

Private Sub FilePrint_Click(ByVal sender As System.Object, ByVal _
e As System.EventArgs) Handles FilePrint.Click
    printout( )
End Sub

Private Sub FilePreview_Click(ByVal sender As System.Object, _
ByVal e As System.EventArgs) Handles FilePreview.Click
    printPreview( )
End Sub

Private Sub FileExit_Click(ByVal sender As System.Object, ByVal e _
As System.EventArgs) Handles FileExit.Click
    SaveAndExit( )
End Sub

' picks up any changes to the text
Private Sub Workspace_TextChanged(ByVal sender As System._
Object, ByVal e As System.EventArgs) Handles Workspace. _
TextChanged
    saved = False
End Sub

Private Sub PrintDocument1_PrintPage(ByVal sender As System _
.Object,ByVal e As System.Drawing.Printing.PrintPageEventArgs) _
Handles PrintDocument1.PrintPage
    Dim yPos As Single = e.MarginBounds.Top
    Dim xPos As Single = e.MarginBounds.Left
    Dim printFont As Font = Workspace.Font
    Dim myBrush As New SolidBrush(Color.Black)

    e.Graphics.DrawString(Workspace.Text, printFont, myBrush, _
xPos, yPos)
    myBrush.Dispose( )
End Sub
```

```
Private Sub printout( )
    PrintDialog1.Document = PrintDocument1
    If PrintDialog1.ShowDialog( ) = DialogResult.OK Then
        PrintDocument1.Print( )
    End If
End Sub

Private Sub printPreview( )
    PrintPreviewDialog1.Document = PrintDocument1
    PrintPreviewDialog1.ShowDialog( )
End Sub

End Class
```

Exercises

1 Add menus and toolbars to the Calculator and at least one other existing program.

2 Explore the FolderBrowserDialog and the PageSetupDialog. Link the Page Setup to the Print routine to allow your user to control margins, paper size and similar settings.

Summary

- Standard Windows features are easily added to your Visual Basic programs.

- A menu system can be built using the MainMenu control, or a context menu with the ContextMenu control.

- To create a toolbar, you set up a collection of buttons. Images can be added to these by linking to an ImageList.

- The Image Editor is a convenient tool for creating icons and other small images.

- Open, Save, Print and Print Preview dialog box controls offer easy ways to handle standard facilities.

09

text processing

In this chapter you will learn:

- how to use the Clipboard
- about functions for string manipulation
- about font formatting and colour setting
- how to display option status in menus and on toolbars

9.1 Editing

Virtually all Windows applications have Cut, Copy and Paste
commands. These store the cut or copied data in the Clipboard –
an area of memory that is maintained by Windows itself, not the
application. Visual Basic knows about the Clipboard – there is a
Clipboard class which has a set of methods for handling it.

Cut and Copy

Getting data into the Clipboard is simple. RichTextBoxes have a
SelectedText property which is the text (and its formatting) that
is currently highlighted, and the **SetDataObject** method copies
the given text into the Windows Clipboard. This is all you need
for a **copy()** subroutine:

```
Private Sub copy( )
    Clipboard.SetDataObject(Workspace.SelectedText)
End Sub
```

And you use the same line in the **cut**() subroutine, followed by
this simple line to delete the selected text.

```
Workspace.SelectedText = ""
```

Paste

Getting data out of the Clipboard is a little trickier. The problem is that any sort of data can be stored in there, so you really
should check that it is suitable for copying into wherever you
are going to put it.

Clipboard data is of the type **IDataObject**. If we have a variable
of this type, we can copy the Clipboard contents into it and then
check its nature with the **GetDataPresent** method, from the
IDataObject class. This compares the data to a given format
(**DataFormats.Text** in this case) and returns True if it is the same.

```
Dim data As IDataObject = Clipboard.GetDataObject( )
    If data.GetDataPresent(DataFormats.Text) Then …
```

To copy the text from the data object into our *Workspace*, we
use the **GetData** method – this needs to be told the format (and
its **DataFormats.Text** again).

```
Workspace.SelectedText = data.GetData(DataFormats.Text)
```

That line will replace the selected text with the contents of the Clipboard, or if nothing is selected, it will insert the new text at the current cursor position.

We can put these together to make a *paste()* subroutine:

```
Private Sub paste( )
    Dim data As IDataObject = Clipboard.GetDataObject( )
    If data.GetDataPresent(DataFormats.Text) Then
        Workspace.SelectedText = data.GetData(DataFormats.Text)
    End If
End Sub
```

Linking commands and code

The next step is to set up the menu commands and toolbar buttons, and add the code to run the new subroutines.

1 Go to the Design window and edit the main menu.

2 Add a new heading '&Edit', with the options 'Cu&t', '&Copy' and '&Paste'.

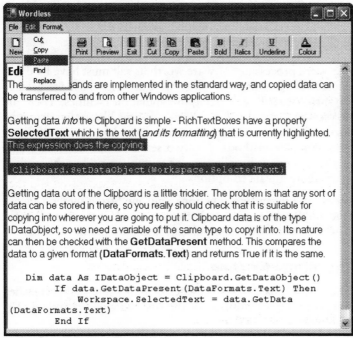

Figure 9.1 Pasting in Wordless.

3 Edit the ImageList, adding Cut, Copy and Paste buttons –
you will find them in the supplied images, along with the
New, Open and Save bitmaps.

4 Edit the Toolbar to add the new buttons. You may also want
to add a separator first – add a button as normal, then select
Separator as the Style.

Keystroke editing

**Having spent all this time getting your Edit commands
working, I'm sure you'll be pleased to know that you don't
need to worry about setting up the keystroke shortcuts,
[Ctrl]-[X] (Cut), [Ctrl]-[C] (Copy) and [Ctrl]-[V] (Paste). They
are already working, automatically. In fact, they would have
been available even if you had not implemented your cut
and paste routines – and they copy the formatting along
with the text, which our routines do not! They are simply
part of a text box's built-in abilities.**

9.2 String manipulation

Any word processing software worth its salt must have Find and
Replace commands, but before we can write those we need to
dip into Visual Basic's string manipulation facilities. There are
two sets of these: the Visual Basic run-time library has around a
dozen functions, and the String class has a larger body of rather
more complex methods. The two sets overlap, and where they
do the function is usually simpler to implement, but the method
offers more advanced options.

We will be using two functions and one String method in our
Find and Replace routines. Let's have a look at those, and glance
at some other string manipulators while we are in the area.

The InStr( ) function

InStr() will look for the presence of one string within another,
and returning the position of the first matching character. The
basic syntax is:

```
position = InStr(start, basetext, searchtext)
```

start is the character position at which to start checking. If this is omitted, the check starts at the beginning. As with all string functions, the first letter is at 1 – this contrasts with String methods, which count letter positions from 0. Here it is at work:

```
Dim basetext As String  = "The quick brown fox"
Dim searchtext As String = "brown"
Dim found As Short
found = InStr(1, basetext, searchtext)
```

After this, *found* will hold 11.

By moving the *start* value forward, you can look for further occurrences of the *searchtext*. For example:

```
Dim basetext As String
Dim searchtext As String
Dim found As Short
Dim start As Short = 1
basetext = "The quick brown fox jumped over the lazy dog"
searchtext = "o"
Do
    found = InStr(start, basetext, searchtext)
    MsgBox("Found at " & found)
    start = found + 1          ' continue from the next character
Loop While start < Len(basetext)
```

The messagebox will show the values 13, 18, 28 and 43.

I've slipped another function in there!

```
Len(text)
```

returns the length of the string.

Case functions

"A" is not the same as "a", but when searching for text, you may not know – or care – the case of the characters. Switching between upper and lower case is easy. There are two functions, and they can be used on single characters or on whole strings.

```
LCase(char)    or    LCase(string)
```
These change the character or string to lower case, e.g.
```
lowertext = Lcase("AbCdEfGhIjKlM")
```
lowertext now holds "abcdefghijklm".

The equivalent upper case functions are:

    UCase(char)   or   LCase(string)

We can combine these with InStr() to produce a case-insensitive search routine:

    found = InStr(start, LCase(basetext), LCase(searchtext))

UCase would work just as well – but don't use one of each!

String slicing

These three functions will copy a chunk from one string into another – the base string is not changed.

    newstring = Mid(basestring, startchar, number)

Mid() is a simple function. It copies *number* characters from *startchar* of *oldstring* into *newstring*. If number is omitted, it copies to the end of the string.

    newstring = Microsoft.VisualBasic.Left(oldstring, number)

This copies *number* characters from the left (start) of *oldstring* into *newstring*. For reasons too complicated to be bothered with, you have to specify Microsoft.VisualBasic when using **Left()**. Mid() is also part of the same library, but you do not need to specify the namespace when using it. **Mid(oldstring, 1,1)** does the same job and is quicker to write.

    newstring = Microsoft.VisualBasic.Right(oldstring, number)

This likewise copies *number* characters from the right-hand end of *oldstring* into *newstring*. **Mid(oldstring, length-number)** will do the same job.

A Proper( ) function

We have now got enough to create a useful **Proper()** function – one that makes sure proper names (of people, places, etc.) have their first character in upper case and the rest in lower case.

First, the one-step-at-a-time version. This uses two local variables to hold the initial letter and the rest of the name – both sliced out of the incoming string by variations on Mid(). They are each forced into the appropriate case, then the two are joined together to feed back into the properly-formed string.

```
Private Function proper(ByVal incoming As String) As String
    Dim initial As String
    Dim rest As String
    initial = Mid(incoming, 1, 1)
    initial = UCase(initial)
    rest = Mid(incoming, 2)
    rest = LCase(rest)
    proper = initial & rest
End Function
```

And here's the compact version. This time LCase() and UCase() are wrapped around the Mid() expressions, and fed to the proper name without going through temporary variables.

```
Private Function proper(ByVal incoming As String) As String
    proper = UCase(Mid(incoming, 1, 1)) & LCase(Mid(incoming, 2))
End Function
```

The Mid( ) statement

There is also a **Mid**() statement which copies text into a string, replacing the existing characters.

```
Mid(oldstring, startchar, number) = newstring
```

For example:

```
Dim oldstring As String
oldstring = "The quick brown fox"
Mid(oldstring, 11, 5) ="black"
MsgBox(oldstring)

Mid(oldstring, 11, 3) = "red"
MsgBox(oldstring)
```

The first messagebox will display "The quick black fox", the second one will display "The quick redck fox". Which points up one of the limitations of this statement – you can only really use it to replace a string with another of the same length. There is a better way of replacing text.

The Replace( ) method

This is a member of the **String** class. It will replace one piece of text with another – of any length – inside a string. The syntax is:

```
newstring = oldstring.Replace(oldtext,newtext)
```

Here's that last example, but with Replace instead of Mid().

```
Dim oldstring As String
Dim newstring As String
oldstring = "The quick brown fox"
newstring = oldstring.Replace("brown", "black")
MsgBox(newstring)

newstring = oldstring.Replace("black", "red")
MsgBox(newstring)
```

This time the messageboxes read "The quick black fox" – as before, and "The quick red fox" – with "red" neatly replacing the longer "black".

Two other String class members that you might find useful are the **IndexOf()** method and the **Length** property.

IndexOf() is equivalent to the **InStr()** function, returning the start position of one string within another.

```
place = basetext.IndexOf(searchtext)
```

Note well that String methods start counting from 0, unlike string functions, where the first character is at 1. For example:

```
Dim basetext As String
Dim searchtext As String
Dim found As Short
basetext = "The quick brown fox"
searchtext = "brown"
found = basetext.IndexOf(searchtext)
```

This will give *found* a value of 10.

Length produces the same results as the Len() function.

```
textLength = basetext.Length
```

If *basetext* held "The quick brown fox", *textLength* would have a value of 19.

For more on the String class methods and properties, look up String class members in the Help system.

9.3 Find and Replace

Let's put these functions and methods to work and develop Find and Replace routines for our word processor.

Find

This revolves around InStr(), which searches the text for the given string, and that part of the routine should need little further explanation.

```
firstChar = InStr(startAt, text, target)
```

This gives us the position of the first character of the matching string, or 0 if there is no match.

The more interesting code is that which deals with the text after it has been found. If there is only a single instance of the found text, we can highlight it by making it the **SelectedText** of *Workspace*. To do this, we need to know where the selection starts and how long it is. The start position is at 1 less than where the match was found (because string functions count from 1, but String members count from 0).

```
Workspace.SelectionStart = firstChar - 1
```

The length is simply the length of the target string:

```
Workspace.SelectionLength = target.Length
```

Setting those two properties defines the **SelectedText**, and it will be shown highlighted when the routine ends.

If we want to be able to find all the occurrences of the matching text, then we need to add two more things to the routine. The first is a loop to keep working through the text. That is straight-forward, though you must remember to move the start position on each time round:

```
startAt = firstChar + 1
```

Highlighting the matches is trickier, as the SelectedText can only be a single area, and also the normal SelectedText highlight does not show up while the routine is working through the loop. The solution offered here is to recolour the text red – the current colour is recorded beforehand, so that it can be restored later.

```
oldcolour = Workspace.SelectionColor
Workspace.SelectionColor = Color.Red
...
Workspace.SelectionColor = oldcolour
```

The full routine follows.

```
Private Sub find( )
    Dim target, text As String
    Dim firstChar As Short = 0
    Dim startAt As Short = 1
    Dim findNext As Short
    Dim oldcolour As Object

    target = InputBox("Text to find", "Find")
    If target = Nothing Then Exit Sub
    text = Workspace.Text
    Do
        firstChar = InStr(startAt, text, target)
        If firstChar = 0 Then
            MsgBox("Not found")
            Exit Do
        Else
            Workspace.SelectionStart = firstChar - 1
            Workspace.SelectionLength = target.Length
            oldcolour = Workspace.SelectionColor
            Workspace.SelectionColor = Color.Red
        End If
        findNext = MsgBox("Find next?", MsgBoxStyle.YesNo, "Find")
        Workspace.SelectionColor = oldcolour
        startAt = firstChar + 1
    Loop Until findNext <> 6
End Sub
```

Replace

All that is really essential here is to collect the text to find and to replace, then apply the **Replace()** method – and as this automatically replaces *every* matching occurrence, we don't even need to worry about running it through a loop.

The routine given here is more complicated than that because I've added some checks. It uses **InStr()**, first to see if the *target* text is there, and then to locate every occurrence of it – these are then recoloured, as in the Find routine. The code then asks for confirmation before doing the replacement.

As it stands, if the user decides not to replace the found strings, this routine leaves them coloured red. You may want to add a further block to run through the text again, and turn them back to the original text colour.

```
Private Sub replace( )
    Dim target, text As String
    Dim newtext As String
    Dim editedtext As String
    Dim firstChar As Short = 0
    Dim startAt As Short = 1
    Dim numChars As Short
    Dim confirm As Short

    target = InputBox("Text to find", "Find and Replace")
    If target = Nothing Then Exit Sub
    numChars = target.Length
    newtext = InputBox("Text to replace it with", "Find and Replace")
    text = Workspace.Text
    firstChar = InStr(startAt, text, target)
    If firstChar = 0 Then
        MsgBox("Not found")
    Else
    ' recolour all occurrences of the matching text
        Do
            Workspace.SelectionStart = firstChar - 1
            Workspace.SelectionLength = target.Length
            Workspace.SelectionColor = Color.Red
            startAt = firstChar + 1
            firstChar = InStr(startAt, text, target)
        Loop Until firstChar = 0
        confirm = MsgBox("Replace all?", MsgBoxStyle.YesNo, _
            "Replace")
        If confirm = 6 Then
            Workspace.Text = text.Replace(target,newtext)
        End If
    End If
End Sub
```

Formatting tools

Before we add the formatting routines, we should get the
menu items and/or toolbar buttons in place so that we can
test them.

The new Format menu is shown in Figure 9.2. This has a
Font Style submenu, with Bold, Italic and Underline options.
These are also present, along with a Colour option, as toolbar
buttons – as normal.

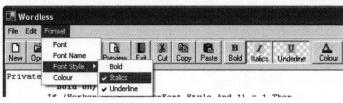

Figure 9.2   The Formatting menu items and toolbar buttons.

9.4 The Font and Color dialog boxes

The Font dialog box makes font formatting ridiculously easy to implement. All you have to do is call up the box and copy the font specification from its Font property into the RichTextBox's Font property.

Place a FontDialog control in the component tray, along with the other dialog boxes, and add the following two lines of code. As this can only be called from the **Format > Font** menu item, the code can be written directly into its **Click** method.

```
Private Sub FormatFont_Click(ByVal sender As System.Object, _
ByVal e As System.EventArgs) Handles FormatFont.Click
    If FontDialog1.ShowDialog( ) = DialogResult.OK Then
        Workspace.SelectionFont = FontDialog1.Font
    End If
End Sub
```

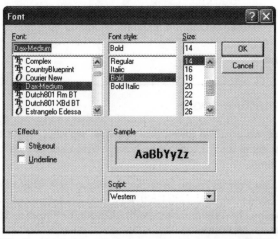

Figure 9.3   The standard Font dialog box can be called up from within Visual Basic.

This is another easy addition. The **ColorDialog** control produces the standard Windows Color dialog box, from which a basic or user-defined colour can be selected.

It is displayed with the usual **ShowDialog()** method, and the result can be found in its **Color** property. As this is to be accessed from a menu option and a toolbar button, its code is written into a new subroutine, which can be called from the menu and toolbar Click methods.

```
Private Sub setColour( )
    If ColorDialog1.ShowDialog( ) = DialogResult.OK Then
        Workspace.SelectionColor = ColorDialog1.Color
    End If
End Sub
```

In this instance, the colour is copied to another Color property. If required it can be stored in a variable of the Object data type.

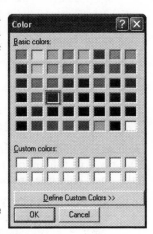

Figure 9.4 The Color dialog box – clicking Define Custom Colors opens the full version of the box.

9.5 FontStyle formatting

You can set the font style options from within the Font dialog box, but we should also offer Bold, Italic and Underline on/off switches – as most word processors do. This will take a little more work. There are two problems to solve.

* The Bold, Italic and Underline switches are all stored in the FontStyle property, and we need to set bits to turn them on and off. We discussed the theory of this in section 4.10.

* If the switches are on, the toolbar buttons should be shown pushed in, and the menu items should be checked.

Xor toggles

The Font.Style property has four components:

> Bold = 1 (when on)
>
> Italics = 2 (when on)
>
> Underline = 4 (when on)
>
> Strikethrough = 8 (when on) – not implemented here

There are predefined constants with these values, which you can use to set single options, e.g. FontStyle.Bold has a value of 1. If we Xor these against the existing Style, it will toggle the options on or off. Suppose Bold and Italics are currently on. Style will have a value of 3. The expression:

```
Workspace.SelectionFont.Style Xor FontStyle.Bold
```

will result in a value of 2 – toggling Bold off.

Look at the bits:

Style	0	0	0	0	0	0	1	1	= Italic on, Bold on
Bold	0	0	0	0	0	0	0	1	
new Style	0	0	0	0	0	0	1	0	= Italic on, Bold off

Do it again, and the result will be 3 as Bold is toggled back on. That gives us this on/off routine – here is the Bold version, the Italic and Underline are basically the same:

```
Private Sub boldOnOff( )
    If Workspace.SelectionFont Is Nothing Then Exit Sub
    newStyle = Workspace.SelectionFont.Style Xor FontStyle.Bold
    setfont( )
End Sub
```

We are not actually setting the font options here. To redefine the font, we have to create a new Font object, with the changed options, and copy that to the text's font. The Font object has three arguments:

```
Font (Family, Size, Style)
```

Family is the font name (you can also use a generic name, e.g. Sans, instead of specifying an exact font). You could define a new font like this:

```
… = New Font ("Arial", 15, FontStyle.Bold)
```

As we only want to set the style, we should pick up the current FontFamily and Size settings from the SelectionFont property.

```
Private Sub setfont()
    Dim MyFont As System.Drawing.Font
    MyFont = Workspace.SelectionFont    'current settings
    Workspace.SelectionFont = New Font(MyFont.FontFamily, _
        MyFont.Size, newStyle)
    formatOnOff()
End Sub
```

Displaying option status

I can't find a neat, compact way of doing this, but the following routine works. It will put a tick by the menu item and show the button as 'pushed' when an option is set.

To find the status of the options, And tests are applied to the Style property with the Bold, Italic and Underline values. If they show an option is on, the menu item's Checked property and the button's Pushed property are both set to True.

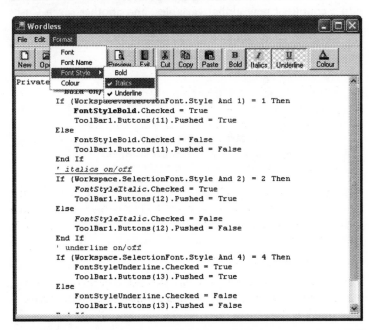

Figure 9.5 The OnOff subroutine – a bit clunky, but it works!

Here's the bold part of the **formatOnOff()** subroutine.

```
If (Workspace.SelectionFont.Style And 1) = 1 Then
    FontStyleBold.Checked = True
    ToolBar1.Buttons(11).Pushed = True
Else
    FontStyleBold.Checked = False
    ToolBar1.Buttons(11).Pushed = False
End If
```

Notice how the toolbar buttons are identified, by using index numbers in the Buttons collection.

The subroutine must be called when the font style settings are changed – i.e. from the **setfont()** subroutine – but also whenever the cursor is moved to a different part of the text. RichTextBoxes have a SelectionChanged() method which picks this up.

9.6 Wordless word processing

This code extends the existing text processor. You will need to add a couple of new global variables, and another seven Cases at the top of the program. The rest can be added after the existing code. Apart from the lines in grey in the first two blocks, only the new code is given here.

```
Public Class Form1
    Inherits System.Windows.Forms.Form
    Dim saved As Boolean
    Dim MyFileName As String = ""
    ' new global variables for Chapter 8
    Dim textColour As Object = System.Drawing.Color.Black
    Dim newStyle As System.Drawing.FontStyle

Private Sub ToolBar1_ButtonClick(ByVal sender As System.Object, _
ByVal e As System.Windows.Forms.ToolBarButtonClickEventArgs) _
Handles ToolBar1.ButtonClick
    Select Case ToolBar1.Buttons.IndexOf(e.Button)
        Case 0
            newFile()
        Case 1
            open()
        Case 2
            save()
```

```
      Case 3
        printout( )
      Case 4
        printPreview( )
      Case 5
        SaveAndExit( )
' new toolbar buttons - 6, 10 and 14 are separators
      Case 7
        cut( )
      Case 8
        copy( )
      Case 9
        paste( )
      Case 11
        boldOnOff( )
      Case 12
        italicOnOff( )
      Case 13
        underlineOnOff( )
      Case 15
        setColour( )
    End Select
End Sub

' use existing code from newFile( ) through to the end

Private Sub cut( )
    Clipboard.SetDataObject(Workspace.SelectedText)
    Workspace.SelectedText = ""
End Sub

Private Sub copy( )
    Clipboard.SetDataObject(Workspace.SelectedText)
End Sub

Private Sub paste( )
    Dim data As IDataObject = Clipboard.GetDataObject( )
    If data.GetDataPresent(DataFormats.Text) Then
        Workspace.SelectedText = data.GetData(DataFormats.Text)
    End If
End Sub

Private Sub EditCut_Click(ByVal sender As System.Object, ByVal _
e As System.EventArgs) Handles EditCut.Click
    cut( )
End Sub
```

```vbnet
Private Sub EditCopy_Click(ByVal sender As System.Object, ByVal _
e As System.EventArgs) Handles EditCopy.Click
    copy()
End Sub

Private Sub EditPaste_Click(ByVal sender As System.Object, ByVal _
e As System.EventArgs) Handles EditPaste.Click
    paste()
End Sub

Private Sub find()
    Dim target, text As String
    Dim firstChar As Short = 0
    Dim startAt As Short = 1
    Dim findNext As Short
    Dim oldcolour As Object

    target = InputBox("Text to find", "Find")
    If target = Nothing Then Exit Sub
    text = Workspace.Text
    Do
        firstChar = InStr(startAt, text, target)
        If firstChar = 0 Then
            MsgBox("Not found")
            Exit Do
        Else
            Workspace.SelectionStart = firstChar - 1
            Workspace.SelectionLength = target.Length
            oldcolour = Workspace.SelectionColor
            Workspace.SelectionColor = Color.Red
        End If
        findNext = MsgBox("Find next?", MsgBoxStyle.YesNo, "Find")
        Workspace.SelectionColor = oldcolour
        startAt = firstChar + 1
    Loop Until findNext <> 6
End Sub

Private Sub replace()
    Dim target, text As String
    Dim newtext As String
    Dim editedtext As String
    Dim firstChar As Short = 0
    Dim startAt As Short = 1
    Dim numChars As Short
    Dim confirm As Short
```

```
   target = InputBox("Text to find", "Find and Replace")
   If target = Nothing Then Exit Sub
   numChars = target.Length
   newtext = InputBox("Text to replace it with", "Find and Replace")
   text = Workspace.Text
   firstChar = InStr(startAt, text, target)
   If firstChar = 0 Then
      MsgBox("Not found")
   Else
   ' recolour all occurrences of the matching text
      Do
         Workspace.SelectionStart = firstChar - 1
         Workspace.SelectionLength = target.Length
         Workspace.SelectionColor = Color.Red
         startAt = firstChar + 1
         firstChar = InStr(startAt, text, target)
      Loop Until firstChar = 0
      confirm = MsgBox("Replace all?", MsgBoxStyle.YesNo, _
         "Replace")
      If confirm = 6 Then
         Workspace.Text = text.Replace(target,newtext)
      End If
   End If
End Sub

Private Sub EditFind_Click(ByVal sender As System.Object, ByVal
e As System.EventArgs) Handles EditFind.Click
   find( )
End Sub

Private Sub EditReplace_Click(ByVal sender As System.Object,
ByVal e As System.EventArgs) Handles EditReplace.Click
   replace( )
End Sub

' formatting commands
Private Sub boldOnOff( )
   If Workspace.SelectionFont Is Nothing Then Exit Sub
   newStyle = Workspace.SelectionFont.Style Xor FontStyle.Bold
   setfont( )
End Sub

Private Sub italicOnOff( )
   newStyle = Workspace.SelectionFont.Style Xor FontStyle.Italic
   setfont( )
End Sub
```

```
Private Sub underlineOnOff()
  newStyle = Workspace.SelectionFont.Style Xor FontStyle. _
    Underline
  setfont()
End Sub

Private Sub setfont()
  Dim MyFont As System.Drawing.Font
  MyFont = Workspace. SelectionFont
  Workspace.SelectionFont = New Font(MyFont.FontFamily, _
    MyFont.Size, newStyle)
  formatOnOff()
End Sub

Private Sub FontStyleBold_Click(ByVal sender As System.Object, _
ByVal e As System.EventArgs) Handles FontStyleBold.Click
  boldOnOff()
End Sub

Private Sub FontStyleItalic_Click(ByVal sender As System.Object, _
ByVal e As System.EventArgs) Handles FontStyleItalic.Click
  italicOnOff()
End Sub

Private Sub FontStyleUnderline_Click(ByVal sender As System. _
Object, ByVal e As System.EventArgs) Handles FontStyleUnderline _
.Click
  underlineOnOff()
End Sub

Private Sub setColour()
  If ColorDialog1.ShowDialog() = DialogResult.OK Then
    Workspace.SelectionColor = ColorDialog1.Color
  End If
End Sub

Private Sub FormatFont_Click(ByVal sender As System.Object, _
ByVal e As System.EventArgs) Handles FormatFont.Click
  If FontDialog1.ShowDialog() = DialogResult.OK Then
    Workspace.SelectionFont = FontDialog1.Font
  End If
End Sub

Private Sub FormatColour_Click(ByVal sender As System.Object, _
ByVal e As System.EventArgs) Handles FormatColour.Click
  setColour()
End Sub
```

```
Private Sub Workspace_SelectionChanged(ByVal sender As _
Object, ByVal e As System.EventArgs) Handles Workspace._
SelectionChanged
   formatOnOff( )
End Sub

Private Sub formatOnOff( )
   ' bold on/off
   If (Workspace.SelectionFont.Style And 1) = 1 Then
      FontStyleBold.Checked = True
      ToolBar1.Buttons(11).Pushed = True
   Else
      FontStyleBold.Checked = False
      ToolBar1.Buttons(11).Pushed = False
   End If
   ' italics on/off
   If (Workspace.SelectionFont.Style And 2) = 2 Then
      FontStyleItalic.Checked = True
      ToolBar1.Buttons(12).Pushed = True
   Else
      FontStyleItalic.Checked = False
      ToolBar1.Buttons(12).Pushed = False
   End If
   ' underline on/off
   If (Workspace.SelectionFont.Style And 4) = 4 Then
      FontStyleUnderline.Checked = True
      ToolBar1.Buttons(13).Pushed = True
   Else
      FontStyleUnderline.Checked = False
      ToolBar1.Buttons(13).Pushed = False
   End If
End Sub
End Class
```

Exercises

1 Find out about drag and drop editing and implement it in the
   text editor. (The Help system is very good on this topic.)

2 A palindrome is a word or phrase that reads the same left to
   right and right to left, e.g. "rats live on no evil star" or
   'Madam I'm Adam". (Note that case, spaces and punctuation are ignored.) Create a function that will return True if a
   string is a palindrome.

3 Let's code some coding. Proper cryptography is complex, so
   we'll make do with letter-shifting – moving the characters a
   set number of places up the ASCII code, so 'Basic' would
   become 'Fewmg' if 4 was the code number. Write routines
   encode and decode text in the text editor.

Summary

- Cut, Copy and Paste commands can be implemented
  using the Windows Clipboard.

- Visual Basic has many ready-made functions for string
  manipulation, including Instr( ), Lcase( ), Ucase( ) and
  Mid( ).

- We can write our own Find and Replace routines, or use
  the Replace( ) method.

- The standard Font and Color dialog boxes can be brought
  into your programs.

- When setting FontStyle, you can toggle individual
  elements on and off using Xor.

- If a toolbar button is being used as a toggle switch, it
  can be made to appear pushed in to show that it is on.

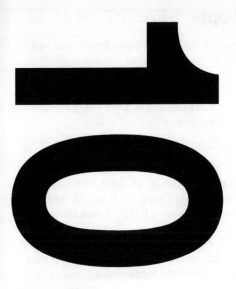

10

graphics and animation

In this chapter you will learn:

- about the graphics object
- how to draw lines and shapes
- about timers and how they can be used to animate images

10.1 Basic concepts

To produce any kind of graphic image in Visual Basic, you have to work through three stages:

1 Create an object on which to draw.

2 Draw the image – there is a set of methods for drawing lines, circles, rectangles and other shapes.

3 Display the object, with its image.

For the most part, you will be working with the properties and methods of the **System.Drawing** namespace, and in particular the **Graphics**, **Color**, **Brush** and **Pen** classes. If you put this line at the very top of your program – above Public Class Form1...

    Imports System.Drawing

... then you won't have to type **System.Drawing** every time that you use a method or property from the namespace.

Let's have a look at the stages in more detail.

The graphics object

This defines the variable *canvas* as a graphics object – note that **System.Drawing** is essential here, even if you have imported it:

    Dim canvas as System.Drawing.Graphics

This must then be associated with a form, so there is a control on which to draw. *Me*, you will remember, is the current form.

    canvas = Me.CreateGraphics()

The two lines can be run together:

    Dim canvas as System.Drawing.Graphics = Me.CreateGraphics()

The graphics area has its origin (0, 0) at the top left corner of the form, and coordinates are given in pixels.

Drawing

The simplest of the drawing methods is DrawLine(), which draws a straight line. The syntax is:

    GraphicsArea.DrawLine(pen, x1, y1, x2, y2)

x1, *y1*, *x2*, *y2* simply define the start and end points of the line. Remember that the coordinates are given in pixels, counting from the top left.

The *pen* is a rather more complex concept – it is an object which sets the colour and width of the line. You can use the Pens class to define the pen directly in the arguments, but this only sets the colour – the width will be 1 pixel, e.g.

```
canvas.DrawLine(Pens.Coral, 50, 50, 150, 200)
```

This draws a thin pale blue line from 50, 50 to 150, 200.

You have more control over the pen if you define it beforehand. Use the **New** constructor to create a new object, setting the colour and width. The pen can then be used in the DrawLine().

```
Dim myPen As New Pen(Color.Red,5)
canvas.DrawLine(myPen, 0, 0, 250, 200)
```

This produces a 5-pixel thick red line from 0, 0 to 250, 200.

Painting the screen

The Drawing methods define the shape on the graphics area, but these alone do not make the image appear on the screen. To make it visible we have to do the drawing in, or call the drawing subroutine from, the **OnPaint()** base method – you will find it it the **Overrides** group in the Class list in the Code window. OnPaint() is called whenever the screen needs 'repainting'.

Put it all together, and we have this code.

```
Protected Overrides Sub OnPaint(ByVal e As PaintEventArgs)
    Dim canvas as System.Drawing.Graphics = Me.CreateGraphics()
    Dim myPen As New Pen(Color.Red,5)
    canvas.DrawLine(myPen, 0, 0, 250, 200)
End Sub
```

In practice, you will get a neater and easier to read program if you write the drawing code inside subroutines, and call those from OnPaint().

```
Protected Overrides Sub OnPaint(ByVal e As PaintEventArgs)
    myDrawingCode()
End Sub
```

10.2 The Drawing methods

The Graphics class has nearly 70 methods. The 10 covered in this chapter demonstrate the main principles behind Graphics methods – explore the others as and when you need them.

Clear( )

The simplest is **Clear**(). This fills the graphics area with a flat colour – typically the background colour – erasing any drawing.

The syntax is:

```
canvas.Clear(colour)
```

Where *canvas* is the graphics area, e.g.

```
canvas.Clear(Color.White)
```

DrawEllipse( ) and DrawRectangle( )

I have put these two together as they are almost identical. The syntax is almost the same as DrawLine().

```
GraphicsArea.DrawEllipse(pen, x, y, width, height)

GraphicsArea.DrawRectangle(pen, x, y, width, height)
```

x, *y*, *width*, *height* define the top left corner and the size of the rectangle itself, or of the rectangle in which the ellipse can be drawn. e.g.

```
Dim myPen As New Pen(Color.Blue,2)
canvas.DrawRectangle(myPen, 50, 50, 200, 400)
canvas.DrawEllipse(myPen, 100, 100, 300, 300)
```

These lines draw a rectangle 200 pixels wide and 400 high, with its top left at 50,50; and a circle 300 pixels in diameter (because it will fit in a box 300 by 300), with the top left of its bounding rectangle at 100,100.

DrawArc( )

An arc is a segment of an ellipse, so it's not surprising that the **DrawArc**() method is an extended version of DrawEllipse. The syntax is:

```
GraphicsArea.DrawEllipse(pen, x, y, width, height, start,sweep)
```

x, y, width, height define the bounding rectangle that the whole ellipse would need.

start is the angle at which the arc begins. This is measured in degrees, counting clockwise and starting from 3 o'clock.

sweep is the angle of the arc.

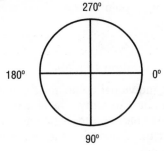

Some examples of arcs.

```
canvas.DrawArc(blackPen, 50, 50, 200, 200, 0, 270)
canvas.DrawArc(blackPen, 300, 50, 100, 200, 180, 135)
canvas.DrawArc(blackPen, 175, 300, 200, 100, 30, 90)
```

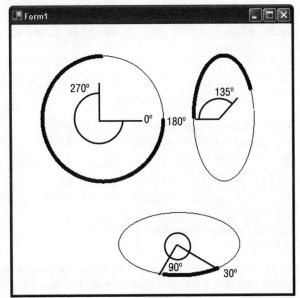

Figure 10.1 The arcs produced by the example lines – these have been drawn over full ellipses of the same size and the angles added.

DrawPolygon( )

This is a rather more complex method. A polygon is defined by the position of its vertices, and these are given in *points* and held in an array. Both need some explanation.

In Visual Basic, a point is a data structure, consisting of a pair of x, y values. To set up a point, use the New constructor, giving the coordinates, e.g.

```
Dim p1 = New Point(100, 50)
```

p1 now refers to the location 100, 50.

Having created the individual points for the polygon, you then have to collect them into an array. The best way to do this is to copy the points at the time of setting up the array. The line should look something like this – note that the values for the array are enclosed in curly brackets:

```
Dim PolyPoint As Point( ) = {p1, p2, p3, p4, p5, p6}
```

This array is then passed to DrawPolygon as an argument, e.g.

```
canvas.DrawPolygon(myPen, PolyPoint)
```

This subroutine will draw a hexagonal polygon, with sides of 100 pixels, centred at 200, 200. It should be called from the OnPaint() subroutine.

```
Public Sub poly( )
    Dim canvas As System.Drawing.Graphics = Me.CreateGraphics()
    Dim myPen As New Pen(Color.Blue, 5)

    Dim p1 = New Point(200, 100)
    Dim p2 = New Point(286, 150)
    Dim p3 = New Point(286, 250)
    Dim p4 = New Point(200, 300)
    Dim p5 = New Point(113, 250)
    Dim p6 = New Point(113, 150)
    Dim PolyPoint As Point( ) = {p1, p2, p3, p4, p5, p6}
    canvas.DrawPolygon(myPen, PolyPoint)
End Sub
```

You might like to know that you can calculate the vertices of any regular polygon using the following formulae.

```
x = Int(xcentre + Sin(vertex * 2 * PI / sides) * size)
y = Int(ycentre + Cos(vertex * 2 * PI / sides) * size)
```

Where *xcentre* and *ycentre* are the coordinates of the centre of the polygon; *vertex* is the position number of the vertex, counting anticlockwise from 0; *sides* is how many sides there are; and *size* is the length of a side.

e.g. these find the coordinates of the third point of a 5-sided polygon, centred at 100, 100 with sides of 50 pixels:

```
x = Int(100 + Sin(3* 2 * PI / 5) * 50)
y = Int(100 + Cos(3* 2 * PI / 5) * 50)
```

Filled shapes

The **Fill...** methods are almost identical to their **Draw...** equivalents. The shapes themselves are defined in exactly the same way. The only real difference is that you use a *pen* to draw a shape, but a *brush* to fill it with colour.

There are several types of brushes, from the simplest, which fill a shape with a flat colour, through to gradient colourings and textured fill. In the next example you will see the SolidBrush and HatchBrush in use.

To set up a solid brush, you just need to supply the colour in the New constructor.

```
Dim myBrushS As New SolidBrush(Color.Red)
```

The HatchBrush belongs to the Drawing2D class, so that must be imported or specified in the line. When creating a new one, you need to specify the hatch style, and the foreground and background colours – in that order. Hatch styles are easily handled – type 'Drawing2D.HatchStyle.' and the list of possible settings will be presented to you.

```
Dim myBrushH As New Drawing2D.HatchBrush(Drawing2D. _
HatchStyle.DashedHorizontal, Color.Green, Color.Yellow)
```

Type the following lines into your OnPaint method. They will draw a filled and an outline rectangle and ellipse.

```
Dim canvas As System.Drawing.Graphics = Me.CreateGraphics()
Dim myBrushS As New SolidBrush(Color.Red)
Dim myBrushH As New Drawing2D.HatchBrush(Drawing2D. _
HatchStyle.DashedHorizontal, Color.Green, Color.Yellow)
Dim myPen As New Pen(Color.Black, 4)
canvas.FillRectangle(myBrushS, 50, 50, 150, 125)
```

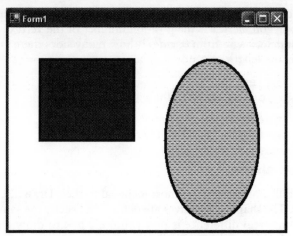

Figure 10.2 Examples of filled shapes, using a SolidBrush and HatchBrush.

```
canvas.DrawRectangle(myPen, 50, 50, 150, 125)
canvas.FillEllipse(myBrushH, 250, 50, 150, 250)
canvas.DrawEllipse(myPen, 250, 50, 150, 250)
myBrushS.Dispose( )
myBrushH.Dispose( )
myPen.Dispose( )
canvas.Dispose( )
```

FillPolygon() is likewise the same as **DrawPolygon()** and **FillPie()** is the equivalent of **DrawArc()**. Substitute a brush for the pen, and define the shape as in the Draw…

Dispose( )

Notice the **Dispose()** methods at the end of some of these drawing examples.

```
myBrushH.Dispose( )
myPen.Dispose( )
canvas.Dispose( )
```

Each new object takes up memory, and to avoid the steady erosion of space as the program runs, you should use **Dispose()** to free the memory once the object has been used.

10.3 DoodlePad – a drawing program

This next example puts some of the drawing techniques to work. It is a very basic program. The drawing is done with the FillRectangle method, which can produce a good solid line – or a series of dots if you move the mouse quickly. FillEllipse or DrawLine could be used equally well. You might want to extend the program to give those as optional 'brush' shapes. You might also want to add a toolbar, instead of or as well as the menu used here.

Note the use of the overridable methods – OnMouseDown, OnMouseMove and OnMouseUp. In the Down and Up subroutines, the *active* variable is switched on and off. When the mouse is moved, if active is off, nothing happens; if it is on, a rectangle is drawn at the current cursor location.

To create this program, you need a blank form to which you have added a MainMenu and a ColorDialog control. The menu should have these items, with names to match their places in the structure, e.g. *FileClear*.

Header	File	Mode	Colour	Line
Items	Clear	Draw	Background	Thin
...	Exit	Eraser	Brush	Regular
...				Wide

Here's DoodlePad!

```
Imports System.Drawing
Public Class Form1
Inherits System.Windows.Forms.Form

    Dim active As Boolean = False
    Dim x1, y1, x2, y2 As Short
    Dim ink As Color = Color.Black
    Dim myBrush As New SolidBrush(Color.Black)
    Dim BrushWidth As Short = 4
    Dim backcolour As Color = Color.White
    Dim canvas As System.Drawing.Graphics

#Region " Windows Form Designer generated code "

Private Sub Form1_Load(ByVal sender As System.Object, ByVal e _
As System.EventArgs) Handles MyBase.Load
    canvas = Me.CreateGraphics()
```

```
End Sub
Protected Overrides Sub OnMouseDown(ByVal e As System. _
Windows.Forms.MouseEventArgs)
    active = True
End Sub

Protected Overrides Sub OnMouseMove(ByVal e As System. _
Windows.Forms.MouseEventArgs)
    If Not active Then Exit Sub
    x1 = e.X
    y1 = e.Y
    canvas.FillRectangle(myBrush, x1, y1, BrushWidth, BrushWidth)
End Sub

Protected Overrides Sub OnMouseUp(ByVal e As System. _
Windows.Forms.MouseEventArgs)
    active = False
End Sub

Private Sub FileClear_Click(ByVal sender As System.Object, ByVal _
e As System.EventArgs) Handles FileClear.Click
    canvas.Clear(backcolour)
End Sub
```

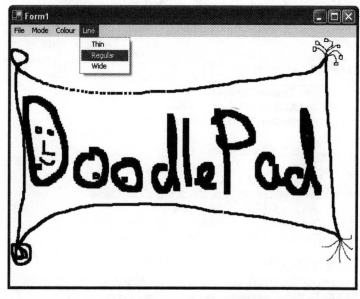

Figure 10.3 DoodlePad in use. Don't draw up at the top left as the menus erase the underlying area when they are opened! This is another limitation of this simple program.

```vbnet
As System.EventArgs) Handles FileExit.Click
    End
End Sub

Private Sub ModeEraser_Click(ByVal sender As System.Object, _
ByVal e As System.EventArgs) Handles ModeEraser.Click
    myBrush.Color = backcolour
End Sub

Private Sub ModeDraw_Click(ByVal sender As System.Object, ByVal _
e As System.EventArgs) Handles ModeDraw.Click
    myBrush.Color = ink
End Sub

Private Sub LineThin_Click(ByVal sender As System.Object, ByVal _
e As System.EventArgs) Handles LineThin.Click
    BrushWidth = 1        'set your own widths
End Sub

Private Sub LineRegular_Click(ByVal sender As System.Object, _
ByVal e As System.EventArgs) Handles LineRegular.Click
        BrushWidth = 4
End Sub
Private Sub LineWide_Click(ByVal sender As System.Object, ByVal _
e As System.EventArgs) Handles LineWide.Click
        BrushWidth = 10 'as wide as you like
End Sub

Private Sub ColourBack_Click(ByVal sender As System.Object, _
ByVal e As System.EventArgs) Handles ColourBack.Click
    If ColorDialog1.ShowDialog() = DialogResult.OK Then
        backcolour = ColorDialog1.Color
    End If
End Sub

Private Sub ColourBrush_Click(ByVal sender As System.Object,
ByVal _ e As System.EventArgs) Handles ColourBrush.Click
    If ColorDialog1.ShowDialog() = DialogResult.OK Then
        ink = ColorDialog1.Color
        myBrush.Color = ink
    End If
End Sub

End Class
```

10.4 Timers

The Timer control enables you to set up code to be executed at timed intervals. It has only one significant method, **Tick**(), and two significant properties:

♦ **Enabled** must be set to True to activate the Timer.

♦ **Interval** defines the time between the executions of the Tick() method. The time is measured in 1/1000 of a second.

Here's a minimal demonstration. It uses a Timer and the system's own clock – accessed through the **TimeOfDay** function, to set up a digital clock display.

1 On a form place a **Label** and a **Timer** – it will drop into the component tray.

2 Give the Label a name, *MyClock* or something similar.

3 Select the Timer and in its Properties display, set **Enabled** to **True** and the **Interval** to 1000 (= 1 second).

4 Double-click on the Timer to open the Code window at its **Tick**() method. Type in this single line:

```
MyClock.Text = TimeOfDay        'MyClock is the label
```

5 Build and run the program. You should have a clock display, updated every second.

10.5 Animation

Here is a more interesting use for a Timer! Try this. It bounces a ball around the screen. Not very exciting, but at least it's moving and it takes very little code. You will need a picture of a ball (if you haven't got one, draw a coloured circle in Paint, select it and save it as a file with **Edit > Copy To**).

Movement is created by adding x and y values to the Left and Top of the ball at each Tick(). When it reaches an edge, the x or y value (as appropriate) is multiplied by −1 to switch it from positive to negative, or vice versa.

1 Place a PictureBox on a form. Specify the ball as its Image, and make sure it fits snugly. Note its width and height.

2 Click onto the form and note its width and height. If the ball is to bounce off the edges of the window, its right-hand limit is the form's width minus the ball's width. The lower limit is the form's height minus the ball's height minus 32, i.e. the thickness of the title bar.

3 Place a Timer in the component tray. Set Enable to True and the Interval to around 20 (adjust the time later when you have seen it in action).

4 Go to the Code window and declare these global variables at the top of the program.

```
Dim ballx, bally As Short
```

5 In the Form_Load subroutine, write these lines to give ballx and bally random values.

```
ballx = Int(Rnd( ) * 20) – 10
bally = Int(Rnd( ) * 20) – 10
```

6 Double-click on the timer to open the Code window at its Tick method and type in the code as shown here – adjusting the limit values to suit the sizes of your ball and form.

```
Private Sub Timer1_Tick(ByVal sender As System.Object, ByVal e _
As System.EventArgs) Handles Timer1.Tick
    ball.Top += bally
    ball.Left += ballx
    If ball.Top > 320 Or ball.Top < 0 Then bally *= -1
    If ball.Left > 552 Or ball.Left < 0 Then ballx *= -1
End Sub
```

7 Build and run.

Animated images

This little program produces a very simple animation of an old banger rattling across the screen. A PictureBox, called *movingCar*, is moved across the screen. As it moves, its image is cycled through three pictures of a car, with variations in the wheels and exhaust smoke. Its vertical position wobbles up and down to add to the impression of movement.

You will need three slightly different pictures of a car – or whatever you want to animate – for this program.

The animation itself is very easily handled, as you will see in a moment. The trickiest part in developing this program was getting the images into it, so that they could be animated. Loading and reloading image files is not a good solution, as the time it takes to access a disk can slow down the animation. Here the images are loaded into PictureBoxes – with **Visible** set to **False** – at design time. These are then copied into the *car()* Image array when the program first starts, by lines like this:

```
car(0) = carPic1.Image
```

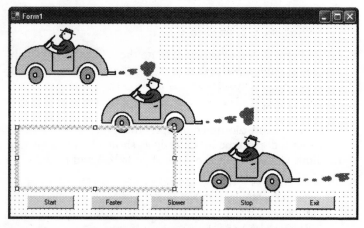

Figure 10.4 The form with the PictureBoxes loaded with their images.

The variable *picnum* is cycled through the values 0, 1 and 2, which are used to select a *car()* image for use in the *movingCar* display. These are the lines that control the changing image.

```
picNum += 1
If picNum = 3 Then picNum = 0
movingCar.Image = car(picNum)
```

The car is moved right to left across the window by subtracting 10 from the Left value. You have to decide what to do when the car reaches the edge. I've allowed it to disappear off one side and reappear on the other. These figures work on my display – adjust yours to suit your image.

```
movingCar.Left -= 10
If movingCar.Left < -200 Then movingCar.Left = 800
```

A random shift up or down increases the illusion of movement.

This formula produces a value in the range –4 to +4.

```
movingCar.Top += Int(Rnd( ) * 9) - 4     'wobble up and down
```

The buttons allow the user to change the speed and to start and stop the vehicle. The speed is adjusting the Timer interval. This must not be allowed to fall to or below 0 as that will crash the system. Starting and stopping is effected by turning the Enabled property on and off.

```
Public Class Form1
    Inherits System.Windows.Forms.Form
    Dim picNum As Short = 0
    Dim car(3) As Image

#Region " Windows Form Designer generated code "

Private Sub Form1_Load(ByVal sender As System.Object, ByVal e _
As System.EventArgs) Handles MyBase.Load
    car(0) = carPic1.Image
    car(1) = carPic2.Image
    car(2) = carPic3.Image
    movingCar.Image = carPic1.Image
    Timer1.Interval = 300                ' set initial speed
End Sub

Private Sub Timer1_Tick(ByVal sender As System.Object, ByVal e _
As System.EventArgs) Handles Timer1.Tick
    ' move the car to the left
    movingCar.Left -= 10
    If movingCar.Left < -200 Then movingCar.Left = 800
    movingCar.Top += Int(Rnd( ) * 9) - 4    'wobble up and down

    ' cycle through the image array
    picNum += 1
    If picNum = 3 Then picNum = 0
    movingCar.Image = car(picNum)
End Sub

Private Sub ExitBut_Click(ByVal sender As System.Object, ByVal _
e As System.EventArgs) Handles ExitBut.Click
    End
End Sub

Private Sub Faster_Click(ByVal sender As System.Object, ByVal _
e As System.EventArgs) Handles Faster.Click
    If Timer1.Interval > 50 Then Timer1.Interval -= 50
End Sub
```

```
Private Sub Slower_Click(ByVal sender As System.Object, ByVal _
e As System.EventArgs) Handles Slower.Click
    Timer1.Interval += 50
End Sub

Private Sub StartBut_Click(ByVal sender As System.Object, ByVal _
e As System.EventArgs) Handles StartBut.Click
    Timer1.Enabled = True
End Sub

Private Sub StopBut_Click(ByVal sender As Object, ByVal e As _
System.EventArgs) Handles StopBut.Click
    Timer1.Enabled = False
End Sub

End Class
```

Figure 10.5 Sorry, couldn't find a way to animate this screenshot. You'll have to implement the program to see how it works!

Online samples

The project and image files for this and other longer programs are available from the TY Visual Basic pages at my Web site. Go to http://homepages.tcp.co.uk/~macbride

Exercises

1 Produce a pie chart to display these values: 35, 27, 23, 10, 5.

2 Code this game. You need a target image, no more than 50 × 50 on a form 600 × 600. Use a timer to set its position at a new random point every second or so. If the user clicks on it, add one to the score, reduce the timer interval and reposition the target. If it has not been clicked when the timer ticks, then the interval should be increased. Display the score and the interval. (The lowest I can get the timer interval down to is 550 – but I'm not a gamer!)

Summary

+ To draw on the screen, you need a graphics object, and you must ensure that the screen is repainted after any drawing.

+ There are methods to draw open or filled lines, rectangles, ellipses, arcs and polygons.

+ To draw lines you need a pen; to fill shapes you need a brush.

+ Objects should be disposed of after use, to save memory.

+ Timers allow you to make events occur at defined intervals.

+ You can animate images using timer-controlled routines.

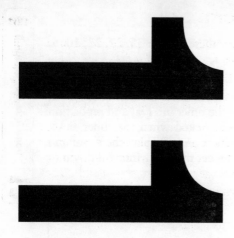

multiple forms

In this chapter you will learn:

- how to create and use additional forms
- about modules and global variables
- about MDI forms and the parent–child relationship

11.1 The second form

So far all our projects have been built in a single form and run in a single window, but one of the features of Windows programs is that they can run any number of separate windows outside or within the main application window. This is managed in Visual Basic by adding extra forms, and it can be done in two ways:

- With the second and subsequent forms opening outside the main form. These are dependent on the main form – you can open and close secondary forms without affecting anything else, but if the main form is closed, the application ends. The Save, Open and other dialog boxes are actually forms of this type.

- With additional forms opening inside the main form, as document windows. These are MDI (Multiple Document Interface) forms, and have a distinct *parent–child* relationship

In either case, similar techniques are used for setting up and handling multiple forms, but MDI forms are slightly more work to set up, while free-standing forms are a bit trickier to manage.

To add a form:

1 In the **Solution Explorer**, right-click on the project name. In the context menu, point to **Add** and select **Add Windows Form…**

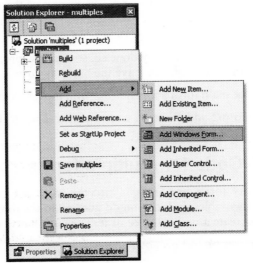

2 In the **Add New Item** dialog box, check that **Windows Form** is selected.

3 If you wish to give the form a more meaningful name, do so – if you have several forms, renaming them is a good idea.

4 Click **Open**.

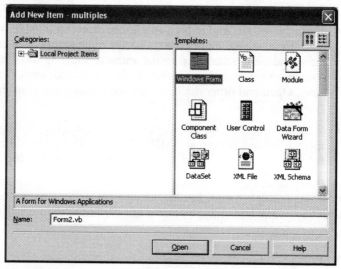

The form can then have controls added as needed, just as with a normal form. Though the form is now part of the project, it is not yet linked to the main form. This is done through the code. Let's try it.

1 If you have not already done so, start a new project and add a form to it – you can leave the name as *Form2*.

2 On the main form add a button, with the text 'Go to Form2'.

3 On Form2 add a button with the text, 'Back to Form1'.

11.2 Code for multiple forms

Secondary forms are brought into the main one by declaring them as variables. In fact, you do not link to the form itself, but instead create a new instance of it. The code has this shape:

```
Dim variable As New Formname
```

If the secondary form is only accessed from one subroutine, then the Dim line can be in that sub, otherwise it should be declared globally at the top of the code or in a module (see section 11.3). In this example, we can write it into the button's Click sub.

Double-click on the button to open the Code window and type:

```
Dim F2 As New Form2     'or whatever you called your form
```

The form can now be referenced through the variable, *F2*. If required, you can read or set the properties of elements on that form from within the main form. For example, you could change the text on the title bar with the line:

```
F2.Text = "The new form"
```

When the program starts, the form will not be visible – it does not in fact exist until created with **Dim**. To make it visible, use the **Show()** or **ShowDialog()** method.

Add this to the button code:

```
F2.Show( )
```

While the window is active, the user can switch between the two by clicking on them.

When you have finished with a secondary form you can Hide() it or Close() it to return to the main form.

Double-click on *Form2*'s button and type this into its Click sub:

```
Me.Hide( )
```

How many forms?

With a straightforward **Dim** declaration, a new instance of the form will be produced if the routine is activated again. This will not be obvious on screen, as the windows will open in exactly the same place every time, directly on top of the existing ones.

If you want to have only one instance of the secondary window, use Static in your declaration.

```
Static Dim F2 As New Form2
```

11.3 Modules and global variables

If there are several secondary forms and you want to be able to pass data between them, or if you want to be able to use the same subroutines or functions from different forms, you need a *module*. This is a separate file, and code stored in here can be accessed from any other part of the project.

To create a module:

1 In the **Solution Explorer**, right-click on the project name. In the context menu, point to **Add** and select **Add Module...**

2 In the **Add New Item** dialog box, select **Module**, change the name if required and click **Open**.

If you want to set up a form so that it can be accessed from anywhere in the project, declare it at the top of the code, using the **Public** keyword instead of **Dim**, e.g.

```
Public F2 as Form2
```

To make a subroutine or function globally-accessible, write it here. Try it. Type in the proper() function that we developed in Chapter 9:

```
Private Function proper(ByVal incoming As String) As String
    proper = UCase(Mid(incoming, 1, 1)) & LCase(Mid(incoming, 2))
End Function
```

Now add a TextBox and a button to each of the forms, adding this code to the button (changing the TextBox name if need be):

```
TextBox1.Text = proper(TextBox1.Text)
```

11.4 A two-form project

This next project is a simple demonstration of an application that uses more than one window. It also shows how you can set up one subroutine so that it handles events generated by several controls. The main form has six PictureBoxes into which images can be loaded from file, and where they are displayed as thumbnails. A click on any PictureBox will open the second form where its image will be displayed full size.

To set up the main form:

1 Start a new project.

2 Place a PictureBox at **Location** (0, 0) of **Size** 160, 120. (If you use a different size, adjust the other locations to suit.)

3 Set these Properties:

Border = FixedSingle
SizeMode = StretchImage
Visible = False

4 Copy the PictureBox. Paste it five times, locating the new boxes at (160, 0), (320, 0), (0, 120), (160, 120) and (320, 120).

5 Set up a menu with two items: **Add Image** and **Exit**.

6 Add an OpenFileDialog – you'll need it for loading images.

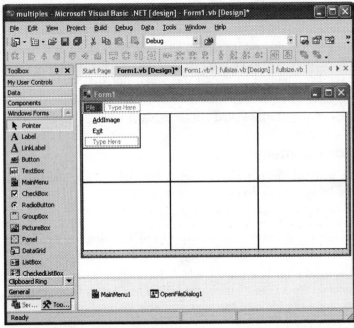

Figure 11.1 The main form with its controls.

To set up the second form:

1 From the **Solution Explorer** add a new form.

2 Place a PictureBox, setting its **SizeMode** to **CenterImage** and **Dock** to **Fill**.

3 Add a button, with the Text 'Close Window'.

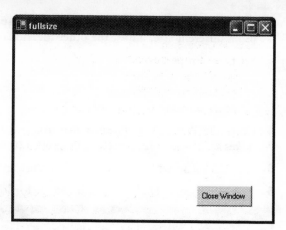

Figure 11.2
The second form.

Let's turn to the code to set this all going. Note that I have named the PictureBoxes as PicBox1 to PicBox6, and the two menu items have been named to match their text, but that otherwise the controls are all at their default names.

Two of the routines need a little explanation.

Adding images

To load an image from file into a PictureBox, you need to use the **Image.FromFile()** method in code like this:

```
PictureBox1.Image = Image.FromFile(filename)
```

To get the filename, we use the **OpenFileDialog**, as we did for text in section 8.5, but setting its Filter to 'Image files | *.bmp'.

The tricky bit is knowing which PictureBox to load it into. I have set up a *count* variable, which is in a Select Case structure to direct the file into the next available PictureBox.

```
Select Case count
    Case 0
        PicBox1.Image = Image.FromFile(filename)
        PicBox1.Visible = True
```

After each addition, the count is incremented, but kept within the range 0 to 5.

```
count += 1
If count > 5 Then count = 0
```

Here's the code for the Form_Load and menu subs for Form1.

```
Public Class Form1
   Inherits System.Windows.Forms.Form
   Dim filename As String
   Dim count As Short

# Windows Form Designer generated code

Private Sub Form1_Load(ByVal sender As System.Object, ByVal e _
As System.EventArgs) Handles MyBase.Load
   count = 0
End Sub

Private Sub FileAddImage_Click(ByVal sender As System.Object, _
ByVal e As System.EventArgs) Handles FileAddImage.Click
   OpenFileDialog1.Filter = "Image files |*.bmp"
   If OpenFileDialog1.ShowDialog = DialogResult.OK Then
      filename = OpenFileDialog1.FileName
   Else
      Exit Sub     ' no image file to add
   End If
   Select Case count
      Case 0
         PicBox1.Image = Image.FromFile(filename)
         PicBox1.Visible = True
      Case 1
         PicBox2.Image = Image.FromFile(filename)
         PicBox2.Visible = True
      Case 2
         PicBox3.Image = Image.FromFile(filename)
         PicBox3.Visible = True
      Case 3
         PicBox4.Image = Image.FromFile(filename)
         PicBox4.Visible = True
      Case 4
         PicBox5.Image = Image.FromFile(filename)
         PicBox5.Visible = True
      Case 5
         PicBox6.Image = Image.FromFile(filename)
         PicBox6.Visible = True
   End Select
   count += 1
   If count > 5 Then count = 0
End Sub
```

```
Private Sub FileExit_Click(ByVal sender As System.Object, ByVal e _
As System.EventArgs) Handles FileExit.Click
    End
End Sub
```

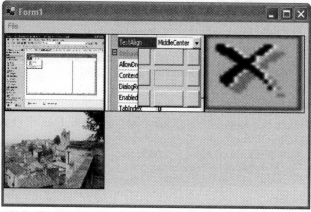

Figure 11.3 The form in action. Only six images can be displayed at any one time, but you can use a larger form, or smaller PictureBoxes and set it up to handle more.

Displaying images on Form2

Once a form has been declared as a variable, its components can be accessed, so the image in PicBox1 could be copied into the PictureBox on the second form and displayed with the lines:

```
f2.PictureBox1.Image = PicBox1.Image
f2.Show()
```

Similar code would then be needed on the other five PictureBoxes. You would also have to think about where to declare the form variable. You could declare *f2* in each of the subroutines, which would give you a new window for every image. If you only wanted the one secondary window, then you would declare it at the top of the code.

There is, however, an alternative approach. We can set up a sub to act as event handler for several controls. Here's how.

1 Go to the Design window for the main form.

2 Double-click on PicBox1 to get into its Click subroutine.

3 At the end of the **Sub** declaration, after '**Handles PicBox1. Click**' add '**, PicBox2.Click, PicBox3.Click...**' and so on.

Notice the commas between the event names.

4 Edit the Sub's name to remind you that it doesn't just handle PicBox1.Click. You should have something like this:

```
Private Sub PicBoxes_Click(ByVal sender As System.Object, ByVal _
e As System.EventArgs) Handles PicBox1.Click, PicBox2.Click, _
PicBox3.Click, PicBox4.Click, PicBox5.Click, PicBox6.Click
```

How do we know which Picbox has been clicked? The answer is in the first parameter *sender*. This identifies the object which generated the Click event. The expression sender.Image will pick the Image property out of the clicked PicBox.

Here's the rest of the code for this subroutine.

```
Dim f2 As New Form2
f2.PictureBox1.Image = sender.Image
f2.Show( )
End Sub
```

The code on Form2

There is not a lot of this. All we need is a **Close**() method on the 'Close Window' button. Here is the entire code for the second form.

```
Public Class Form2
    Inherits System.Windows.Forms.Form

# Windows Form Designer generated code

Private Sub Button1_Click(ByVal sender As System.Object, ByVal _
e As System.EventArgs) Handles Button1.Click
    Me.Close( )
End Sub
End Class
```

11.5 MDI forms

With MDI forms, the main form is known as the *parent*, and a secondary form is referred to as a *child* – and there are properties that control and describe the relationships. When declaring a new child form, for example, it is linked to the parent by a line like this:

```
NewChild.MDIParent = Me        'Me is the parent form
```

The child windows open inside the main window, and this has a number of implications:

- The parent window can have no content, apart from a menu and a toolbar – you must have one or the other to allow you to do anything.

- If there may be more than one child window, you will need routines to manage their layout – but happily there are ready-made commands for the standard Cascade and Tile layouts.

- If you have menus in both the parent and child windows, you will need to ensure that they fit together in some way.

Parent and child forms

To turn a form into a parent form, you simply set its **IsMDIContainer** property to true – you will find it in the Window Style set, towards the bottom of the list.

Do this before you do anything else at all with the form! The central area, where controls are placed, will be emptied – this is the space where the child windows will open.

A child form is created in exactly the same way as an ordinary secondary form. It will become a child only when the form is defined in the code, by setting its **MdiParent** property to *Me* – the defining form. The crucial lines look like this:

```
Dim NewChild As New ChildForm
' set the parent form
NewChild.MdiParent = Me
' display the new form
NewChild.Show( )
```

A child window can be easily accessed from the parent. For example, in the Open routine, you will see this line:

```
NewChild.Workspace.LoadFile(OpenFileDialog1.FileName)
```

This is virtually the same command that we used to load a file into our text editor. The only difference is that the *Workspace* object is prefixed by *NewChild*, the name of the window.

As there can be any number of child windows, you may need to identify which one you are working with. The parent form has an **ActiveMdiChild** property that knows which child is on top. You can see this at work in the Close routine.

```
Private Sub CloseChild( )
    Dim activeChild As Form = Me.ActiveMdiChild
    If activeChild Is Nothing Then Exit Sub
    activeChild.Close( )          'close the window
    activeChild.Dispose( )        ' reclaim the memory
End Sub
```

Menus in MDI forms

In a typical parent–child application you will have two distinct sets of commands. When no child window is open, you only need to be able to open a file, start a new one or exit from the program. Once you have one or more child windows open, you also need to be able to create and edit the document, save the file and manage the window layout.

You can put all your commands in the parent window, and leave the child set disabled until a child window is opened. This works, but there is a neater solution. We can write the commands into a menu on the child form, but merge this with the main form's menu at run-time. It cuts out the need to enable and disable the commands as child windows open and close, but also it lets us place the code *for* the child form *on* the child form. (If your code is trying to access a child form from the main form, it must first work out which child is active, and then include its name when identifying any controls or variables on the form.)

There are two aspects to merging menus:

◆ the menu items which are present in both menus – i.e. the headings – must be put into merge mode;

◆ the items in the merged menus must be given numbers to indicate their order.

An example will show how this works.

1 Set up **File** menus on both forms. On the parent form place the items **New, Open, Close** and **Exit**; on the child form, place **Save** and **Save As**.

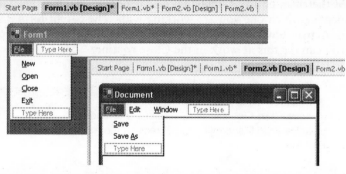

Figure 11.4 Starting to build a merged menu. The menus are created as normal, but with the addition of MergeOrder numbers and with MergeType set to MergeItems.

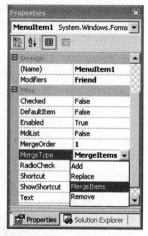

2 On the parent form, select the **File** item. In the Properties window, set its **MergeType** to **MergeItems** and the **MergeOrder** to **1** – this is the first heading across the menu bar.

3 Work down the **File** menu, setting the **MergeOrder** values to **New** = 1, **Open** = 2; **Close** = 3; = 6. These will be their places in the merged **File** menu.

4 On the child form, set the **File** item's **MergeType** to **MergeItems** and the **MergeOrder** to **1** – the same as in the other menu.

5 On the child **File** menu, set these **MergeOrder** values: **Save** = 4 and **Save As** = 5 so that they slot between **Close** and **Exit**.

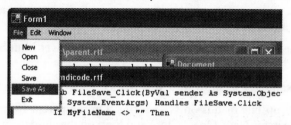

Figure 11.5 The merged menu in the finished program. You will be able to test it once you have written the code to open a child window.

Window management

Visual Basic makes this very simple. For a start, if you have a **Window** menu item in a parent/child program, it will automatically add to it the names of windows as they are opened. Clicking on them will switch control between the windows, as normal. And you do not have to write a single word of code to make this happen!

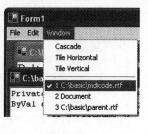

Controlling the layout is not much work either. There are three commands, in the **MdiLayout** set which will arrange the child windows in the **Cascade**, **TileHorizontal** and **TileVertical** layouts. These work on the LayoutMdi property of the parent form, but the code is best written on the child form – as they are to be called up by items on the child's Window menu. The lines should take this shape:

```
Me.ParentForm.LayoutMdi(MdiLayout.Cascade)
```

or

```
Me.ParentForm.LayoutMdi(MdiLayout.TileHorizontal)
```

or

```
Me.ParentForm.LayoutMdi(MdiLayout.TileVertical)
```

11.7 An MDI text editor

The Parent code

This only has code for starting, opening and closing files, and for exiting from the program – everything else is written into the child form.

New and Open are written directly into their menu items' Click event handlers. The close routine has its own Sub, as this is used by both the Close and Exit menu items.

```
Public Class Form1
    Inherits System.Windows.Forms.Form

# Windows Form Designer generated code

Private Sub FileNewChild_Click(ByVal sender As System.Object, _
ByVal e As System.EventArgs) Handles FileNewChild.Click
```

```
      Dim NewChild As New ChildForm    ' declare the form variable
      NewChild.MdiParent = Me    ' set the parent form
      NewChild.Show( )             ' display the new form
   End Sub

   Private Sub FileOpen_Click(ByVal sender As System.Object, ByVal _
   e As System.EventArgs) Handles FileOpen.Click
      OpenFileDialog1.Filter = "Rich Text Format|*.rtf"
      If OpenFileDialog1.ShowDialog( ) = DialogResult.OK Then
         Dim NewChild As New ChildForm  'create a new child
         NewChild.MdiParent = Me
         ' load the file into the child form
         NewChild.Workspace.LoadFile(OpenFileDialog1.FileName)
         NewChild.Text = OpenFileDialog1.FileName
         NewChild.Show( )
      End If
   End Sub

   Private Sub FileCloseChild_Click(ByVal sender As System.Object, _
   ByVal e As System.EventArgs) Handles FileCloseChild.Click
      CloseChild( )
   End Sub

   Private Sub CloseChild( )
      Dim activeChild As Form = Me.ActiveMdiChild
      If activeChild Is Nothing Then Exit Sub
      activeChild.Close( )              'close the window
      activeChild.Dispose( )            ' reclaim the memory
   End Sub

   Private Sub FileExit_Click(ByVal sender As System.Object, ByVal e _
   As System.EventArgs) Handles FileExit.Click
      ' close every child window
      While Not (Me.ActiveMdiChild Is Nothing)
         CloseChild( )
      End While
      End
   End Sub

End Class
```

The Child code

Much of this code is based on the single-window text editor that
we developed in Chapter 8 – and some intelligent cut-and-paste
could save you quite a bit of typing.

```
Public Class ChildForm
    Inherits System.Windows.Forms.Form
    Dim saved As Boolean
    Dim MyFileName As String = ""

# Windows Form Designer generated code

Private Sub FileSave_Click(ByVal sender As System.Object, ByVal _
e As System.EventArgs) Handles FileSave.Click
    If MyFileName <> "" Then
        Workspace.SaveFile(MyFileName)  ' resave current file
        saved = True
    Else
        SaveAs()      ' go to the Save dialog box
    End If
End Sub

Private Sub FileSaveAs_Click(ByVal sender As Object, ByVal e As _
System.EventArgs) Handles FileSaveAs.Click
    SaveAs()
End Sub

Private Sub SaveAs()
    SaveFileDialog1.Filter = "Rich Text Format|*.rtf"
    SaveFileDialog1.Title = "Save document"
    If SaveFileDialog1.ShowDialog() = DialogResult.OK Then
        Workspace.SaveFile(SaveFileDialog1.FileName)
        MyFileName = SaveFileDialog1.FileName
        Me.Text = MyFileName
        saved = True
    End If
End Sub

Private Sub CheckSave()
    Dim saveNow As Short
    If Not saved Then
        saveNow = MsgBox("Do you want to save the document?", _
3, "Save file?")
        If saveNow = 6 Then SaveAs()
    End If
End Sub

Private Sub EditCut_Click(ByVal sender As Object, ByVal e As _
System.EventArgs) Handles EditCut.Click
    Clipboard.SetDataObject(Workspace.SelectedText)
    Workspace.SelectedText = ""
```

```
End Sub

Private Sub EditCopy_Click(ByVal sender As System.Object, ByVal _
e As System.EventArgs) Handles EditCopy.Click
    Clipboard.SetDataObject(Workspace.SelectedText)
End Sub

Private Sub EditPaste_Click(ByVal sender As Object, ByVal e As _
System.EventArgs) Handles EditPaste.Click
    Dim data As IDataObject = Clipboard.GetDataObject()
    If data.GetDataPresent(DataFormats.Text) Then
        Workspace.SelectedText = data.GetData(DataFormats.Text)
    End If
End Sub

Private Sub WindowCascade_Click(ByVal sender As System.Object, _
ByVal e As System.EventArgs) Handles WindowCascade.Click
    Me.ParentForm.LayoutMdi(MdiLayout.Cascade)
End Sub

Private Sub WindowTileHorizontal_Click(ByVal sender As Object, _
ByVal e As System.EventArgs) Handles WindowTileHorizontal.Click
    Me.ParentForm.LayoutMdi(MdiLayout.TileHorizontal)
End Sub

Private Sub WindowTileVertical_Click(ByVal sender As Object, ByVal _
e As System.EventArgs) Handles WindowTileVertical.Click
    Me.ParentForm.LayoutMdi(MdiLayout.TileVertical)
End Sub

Private Sub Workspace_TextChanged(ByVal sender As System.Object, _
ByVal e As System.EventArgs) Handles Workspace. TextChanged
    saved = False
End Sub

Private Sub ChildForm_Closed(ByVal sender As Object, ByVal e As _
System.EventArgs) Handles MyBase.Closed
CheckSave( )
End Sub

Private Sub ChildForm_Load(ByVal sender As Object, ByVal e As _
System.EventArgs) Handles MyBase.Load
    ' if window was started by Open, the filename is in the title bar
    If Me.Text <> "Document" Then MyFileName = Me.Text
End Sub

End Class
```

Exercises

1 Add a third form to the MDI demo. This one should contain a PictureBox with the Dock property set to Fill. Adapt the code so that it can either load RTF files into the RichTextBox form or image files (*.bmp, *.jpg, *.pcx or *.gif) into the new form.

2 Starting from scratch, create an MDI version of the image viewer.

Summary

* A project can contain any number of forms. The first form always has a special status, either as the main form or as the parent.

* Second and subsequent forms can be opened from the main form with the Show( ) command, and removed with Hide( ) or Close( ).

* If you need to be able to access a variable from several forms, you should declare it globally in a module.

* In MDI forms, the first form is the parent, and subsequent forms are children.

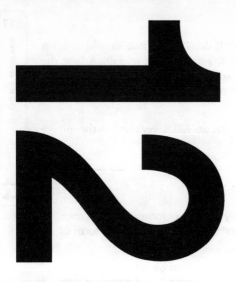

12

answers to exercises

Most programming problems have more that one possible solution. The ones given here are just suggestions to help you if you get stuck.

A few questions are completely open-ended but build on what should be well-established techniques. The simple test with any of these – as with any program – is 'Does it work?'

Chapter 2

1 Private Sub Button1_Click_1(ByVal sender As System.Object, ByVal
    e As System.EventArgs) Handles Button1.Click
        Username.Text = InputBox("Please enter your name")
        Address.Text = InputBox("Address")
        Email.Text = InputBox("Email address")
    End Sub

2 Private Sub OffButton_Click(ByVal sender As System.Object, ByVal _
    e As System.EventArgs) Handles OffButton.Click
        Me.BackColor = Color.Black
        Label1.BackColor = Color.Black
        OnButton.Enabled = True
        OffButton.Enabled = False
    End Sub

The On button code is almost identical.

Chapter 3

1 You just need one line of code in the Scroll subroutines of the
scrollbars. Here's the line for VScrollBar_Scroll:

    PictureBox1.Top = VScrollBar1.Value

2 Your form should have RadioButtons for the Sex and Age
group, and CheckBoxes for the competences.

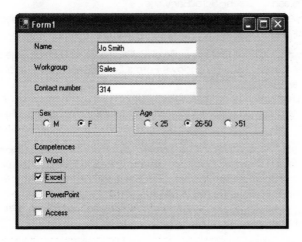

Chapter 4

1
```
Dim fullname As String       '(a) full name in one string, or...
Dim surname As String        'treat separately - you can now
Dim forenames As String      'sort alphabetically by surname

Dim yearOfService As Short   '(b) years of services

Dim phone As String          '(c) not a number for calculating

Dim salary As Double         '(d) Single will do if the MD gets less
                             than £1 million
```

2
```
'at the top of the form
Dim days() As String = {"Sunday", "Monday", "Tuesday", _
"Wednesday", "Thursday", "Friday", "Saturday"}

'in NumericUpDown1_ValueChanged
TextBox1.Text = days(NumericUpDown1.Value)
```

3
```
Private Sub HScrollBar1_Scroll(ByVal sender As System.Object, _
ByVal e As System.Windows.Forms.ScrollEventArgs) Handles _
RedHScrollBar.Scroll
    red = RedHScrollBar.Value
    canvas.BackColor = Color.FromArgb(alpha, red, green, blue)
    'canvas is the PictureBox control
End Sub

Private Sub GreenHScrollBar_Scroll(ByVal sender As System.Object, _
ByVal e As System.Windows.Forms.ScrollEventArgs) Handles _
GreenHScrollBar.Scroll
    green = GreenHScrollBar.Value
    canvas.BackColor = Color.FromArgb(alpha, red, green, blue)
End Sub

Private Sub BlueHScrollBar_Scroll(ByVal sender As System.Object, _
ByVal e As System.Windows.Forms.ScrollEventArgs) Handles _
BlueHScrollBar.Scroll
    blue = BlueHScrollBar.Value
    canvas.BackColor = Color.FromArgb(alpha, red, green, blue)
End Sub

Private Sub AlphaVScrollBar_Scroll(ByVal sender As System.Object, _
ByVal e As System.Windows.Forms.ScrollEventArgs) Handles _
AlphaVScrollBar.Scroll
    alpha = AlphaVScrollBar.Value
    canvas.BackColor = Color.FromArgb(alpha, red, green, blue)
End Sub
```

Chapter 5

1
```
Private Sub StartBtn_Click(ByVal sender As System.Object, ByVal _
e As System.EventArgs) Handles StartBtn.Click
    Dim nth As Short
    Dim trignumber As Integer
    Dim count As Short
    nth = Val(InputBox("Which triangle number?"))
    trignumber = 0
    For count = 1 To nth
        trignumber += count
    Next
    MsgBox("The " & nth & " triangle number is " & trignumber)
End Sub
```

2 Here is a possible solution – note that the direct debit discount can be treated as a separate matter after the age and waged variables have been dealt with.

```
Private Sub members( )
    Dim age As Short
    Dim waged As Boolean
    Dim dd As Boolean
    Dim fee As Short

    age = Val(InputBox("Age"))
    If (MsgBox("Are you a wage-earner", 4 ) = 6) Then waged = True
    If (MsgBox("Pay by direct debit", 4) = 6) Then dd = True
    ' junior members
    If age <= 16 Then
        fee = 20
    'adult members
    Elseif (age > 16) And (age < 65) Then
        If waged Then : fee = 50  ' colon same as using two lines
        Else : fee = 30
        End If
    'over 65 - must be, as rest already found
    Elseif waged Then : fee = 40
    Else : fee = 25
    End If
    'discount for direct debit
    If dd Then fee *= 0.9
    MsgBox("The membership fee will be " & fee)
End Sub
```

3 This is based on the form shown in Figure 5.6. The names of the controls are all based on the Text values shown there. This has many limitations, but it shows the key techniques.

As we need to update the screen in exactly the same way from four points of the program, this has been written into a new subroutine – anticipating the topic of Chapter 6.

```
Imports System.io

Public Class Form1
    Inherits System.Windows.Forms.Form
    Dim username(100) As String
    Dim email(100) As String
    Dim path As String = "C:\temp\addresses.txt"
    Dim current As Short = 0       'item to be displayed
    Dim count As Short
    Dim howmany As Short = 0  'number in array/file

#Windows Form Designer generated code

Private Sub AddBtn_Click(ByVal sender As System.Object, ByVal e _
As System.EventArgs) Handles AddBtn.Click
    Dim onemore As Short
    Do
        username(howmany) = InputBox("Name")
        email(howmany) = InputBox("Email address")
        onemore = MsgBox("Another one?", MsgBoxStyle.YesNo)
        howmany += 1
    Loop While onemore = 6       ' Yes answer
    current = howmany - 1
    updateDisplay( )
End Sub

Private Sub ExitBtn_Click(ByVal sender As System.Object, ByVal e _
As System.EventArgs) Handles ExitBtn.Click
    Dim datafile As StreamWriter = New StreamWriter(path)
    ' write all items to file
    For count = 0 To howmany
        datafile.WriteLine(username(count))
        datafile.WriteLine(email(count))
    Next
    datafile.Close( )
    End
    End Sub

Private Sub Form1_Load(ByVal sender As System.Object, ByVal e _
```

```
As System.EventArgs) Handles MyBase.Load
   If Not (File.Exists(path)) Then Exit Sub
   Dim datafile As StreamReader = File.OpenText(path)
   'read items from file – stop when you reach a blank
   Do
      username(count) = datafile.ReadLine
      email(count) = datafile.ReadLine
      count += 1 'ready for next
   Loop While username(count - 1) <> ""
   datafile.Close()
   howmany = count - 1
   current = 0                        'start to display at first entry
   updateDisplay()
End Sub

Private Sub Previous_Click(ByVal sender As System.Object, ByVal _
e As System.EventArgs) Handles Previous.Click
   'copy values back into array – this saves edits
   username(current) = UserNameBox.Text
   email(current) = EmailBox.Text
   If current > 0 Then current -= 1
   updateDisplay()
End Sub

Private Sub NextBtn_Click(ByVal sender As System.Object, ByVal _
e As System.EventArgs) Handles NextBtn.Click
   username(current) = UserNameBox.Text
   email(current) = EmailBox.Text
   If current < howmany - 1 Then current += 1
   updateDisplay()
End Sub

Private Sub updateDisplay()
   UserNameBox.Text = username(current)
   EmailBox.Text = email(current)
   CurrentBox.Text = current
End Sub

End Class
```

Chapter 6

1 You will need four more buttons, and code like this:

```
'declare at the top
   Dim memory As Double
```

```
'new subs for the memory buttons
Private Sub MemInBtn_Click(ByVal sender As System.Object, ByVal _
e As System.EventArgs) Handles MemInBtn.Click
    memory = Val(DisplayTxt.Text)
    newnum = True        'the next digit starts a new number
End Sub

Private Sub MemOutBtn_Click(ByVal sender As System.Object, _
ByVal e As System.EventArgs) Handles MemOutBtn.Click
    DisplayTxt.Text = memory     'copy into the display
End Sub

Private Sub MemPlusBtn_Click(ByVal sender As System.Object, _
ByVal e As System.EventArgs) Handles MemPlusBtn.Click
    memory += Val(DisplayTxt.Text)
End Sub

Private Sub MemMinusBtn_Click(ByVal sender As System.Object, _
ByVal e As System.EventArgs) Handles MemMinusBtn.Click
    memory -= Val(DisplayTxt.Text)
End Sub
```

2 The new root and power functions fit into the program in the same way as the intPower function.

```
' add to Select Case
    Case 7 : n1 = root(n1, n2)
    Case 8 : n1 = fullpower(n1, n2)


Private Sub RootBtn_Click(ByVal sender As System.Object, ByVal _
e As System.EventArgs) Handles RootBtn.Click
    processOp(7)
End Sub

Private Function root(ByVal base As Double, ByVal exponent As _
Double)
    root = Exp(Log(base) / exponent)
End Function

Private Sub FullPowBtn_Click(ByVal sender As System.Object, ByVal _
e As System.EventArgs) Handles FullPowBtn.Click
    processOp(8)
End Sub

Private Function fullpower(ByVal base As Double, ByVal exponent _
As Double)
    fullpower = Exp(Log(base) * exponent)
End Function
```

Chapter 9

2
```
Private Function palindrome(ByVal word As String) As Boolean
    Dim newword As String = ""
    Dim letter As Char
    Dim reverse As String = ""
    Dim count As Short
    word = Lcase(word)              'convert to lower case
    For count = 1 To Len(word)
        letter = Mid(word, count, 1)
        'cut out all spaces and punctuation
        If (letter >= "a") And (letter >="z") Then newword &= letter
    Next
        'build new word from right to left
    For count = 1 To Len(newword)
        reverse = Mid(newword, count, 1) & reverse
    Next
    palindrome = (reverse = newword )  'gives True of False value
End Function
```

3
```
Private Sub encode( )
    Dim count As Short
    Dim temp As String
    Dim key As Short
    key = InputBox("Code number")
    temp = Workspace.Text
    For count = 1 To Len(temp)
        Mid(temp, count, 1) = Chr(Asc(Mid(temp, count, 1)) + key)
    Next
    Workspace.Text = temp
End Sub
```

The decode routine is exactly the same except that the *key* value is subtracted.

Chapter 10

1 This assumes that you have a graphics area called *canvas*, and then you have imported the Graphics class. The pie is 200 pixels in diameter, with the top left at 100,100.

```
Private Sub pie( )
    Dim slice( ) As Single = {35, 27, 23, 10, 5}
    Dim total As Single = 0
```

```
    Dim count As Short
    Dim start, arc As Single
    For count = 0 To 4
        total += slice(count)          'find the total size of the pie
    Next
    start = 0
    For count = 0 To 4
        arc = slice(count) / total * 360    'the size of each slice
        Select Case count                   'set colours for each slice
            Case 0 : myBrush.Color = Color.Red
            Case 1 : myBrush.Color = Color.Yellow
            Case 2 : myBrush.Color = Color.Blue
            Case 3 : myBrush.Color = Color.Green
            Case 4 : myBrush.Color = Color.Indigo
        End Select
        canvas.FillPie(myBrush, 100, 100, 200, 200, start, arc)
        start += arc                    'move the start position on
    Next
End Sub
```

2 Here is one implementation of the game. Note the use of *hit*
to control whether or not the interval is increased.

```
Public Class Form1
    Inherits System.Windows.Forms.Form
    Dim hit As Boolean
    Dim score As Short
# Windows Form Designer generated code

Private Sub Timer1_Tick(ByVal sender As System.Object, ByVal e _
As System.EventArgs) Handles Timer1.Tick
    relocate( )
End Sub

Private Sub target_Click(ByVal sender As System.Object, ByVal e _
As System.EventArgs) Handles target.Click
    Timer1.Interval -= 50                       'faster next time
    ScoreLbl.Text = Val(ScoreLbl.Text) + 1      'add to score
    IntervalLbl.Text = Timer1.Interval
    hit = True
    relocate( )
End Sub

Private Sub relocate( )
    If Not hit Then Timer1.Interval += 50      'missed, make it slower
    target.Left = Int(Rnd( ) * 500)
```

```
        target.Top = Int(Rnd( ) * 500)
        hit = False
    End Sub

End Class
```

Chapter 11

1 For this, I have renamed the second form as *TextChild*, and added a form called *PicForm* (this contains only a PictureBox called *frame*). After the file has been located, the child forms are opened and their files loaded in two new subroutines newtext() and newimage(). To have left all the code in the one opening routine would have produced very messy code!

```
Private Sub FileOpen_Click(ByVal sender As System.Object, ByVal
e As System.EventArgs) Handles FileOpen.Click
    Dim ext As String
    ' OpenFileDialog1.Filter = "Rich Text Format|*.rtf"
    If OpenFileDialog1.ShowDialog( ) = DialogResult.OK Then
        ext = Microsoft.VisualBasic.Right(OpenFileDialog1.FileName, 3)
        If InStr("rtf doc", ext) > 0 Then
            newtext(OpenFileDialog1.FileName)
        ElseIf InStr("bmp jpg pcx", ext) > 0 Then
            newimage(OpenFileDialog1.FileName)
        End If
    End If
End Sub

Private Sub newtext(ByVal fname As String)
    Dim NewChild As New TextChild
    NewChild.MdiParent = Me
    NewChild.Workspace.LoadFile(fname)
    NewChild.Text = fname
    NewChild.Show( )
End Sub

Private Sub newimage(ByVal fname As String)
    Dim newchild As New PicForm
    newchild.MdiParent = Me
    newchild.frame.Image = Image.FromFile(fname)
    newchild.Text = fname
    newchild.Show( )
End Sub
```

taking it further

This book should have helped to get you started with Visual Basic, but it won't have made you an expert – there's a lot more to learn before you can claim that label!

The Help system in Visual Basic is very comprehensive – in fact, there is so much information that it can take a while to filter the many possible topics to find the one that answers your question. Persevere. The more familiar that you are with Visual Basic, and with its Help system, the easier it becomes to get the Help that you need.

There are many example programs available online from Microsoft, and linked from the Help system. Follow them up and examine them closely to see how experienced programmers handle the code. If you head out of the Help system and into the general World Wide Web, you will again find many sources of advice and lots of sample programs to explore. You should also look up 'visual basic' in the newsgroup subscription routine of your news reader.

But the most important thing that you can do to take your Visual Basic expertise further is to experiment and explore. Be creative! Write some games, utilities, small applications – or large ones – to your own specifications. Don't be afraid to try something new. The worst that can happen is that your brain will start to ache from thinking – and that won't cause lasting damage!

teach
yourself

C++
richard riley

- Are you new to programming?
- Do you need to improve your existing C++ skills?
- Do you want to become an expert programmer?

C++ is a concise guide to programming in C++, one of the most popular and versatile languages in use today. All the concepts and techniques you need to create powerful programs are clearly explained, with examples and revision exercises used throughout.

Richard Riley is a computer programmer who has written extensively in C++, Perl, Java, JavaScript and HTML.